FINDING
THE SAFEST PLACE
ON EARTH

The story of an addict named Jack

Chaplain Patrick Day

The Worst of Times

Jack squeezed his cell phone as if he were trying to strangle a snake. His mother had just hung up on him. If she were there in person, he might have tried to strangle her instead. In a tirade laced with profanities, he muttered several curses and pleas for trucks to run over her or gunmen to take her out.

He'd had no contact with his mother since she walked out the front door the day before he turned four—until he answered the phone three minutes prior. She said, with the voice an assassin might use before firing a fatal shot, "Your father was killed two hours ago by a trucker driving the wrong way on an interstate at 80 miles an hour. They think drugs were involved. There's a pileup of 14 cars and traffic has been blocked in both directions."

Jack shouted into the phone as if he were talking to someone a block away, "What? What's going on? Who is this? What are you saying about my father?"

She knew her message would devastate Jack, like a bullet into his heart, and delivered it with gleeful bitterness. "This is your mother calling. Your father is dead. Thought you'd like to know. Check CNN. It's headline news." She said nothing more. Jack felt like he'd been punched in the stomach, hard. He couldn't breathe and he couldn't talk. His mind locked up into a tight fist. A minute passed in silence. Then she hung up.

Marie had been a free spirit who no longer wanted to be tied down with a family thirty-two years ago. Jack's father gave her money for a couple of years, hoping she'd come back, but stopped payments the day he found out she'd married another man, who ended up to be a ne'er-do-well freeloader. She blamed Jack's father and his worthless son for her subsequent misfortunes. This was her chance to get some revenge.

Immediately, he turned to CNN and saw that what his mother had said was true. He felt sick to his stomach. The father who had taken care of him for 36 years had been killed in an instant.

John, a real estate attorney, devoted his life to raising Jack when Marie left in the middle of the night. He helped him with his schoolwork when it was too hard. He went to every game Jack played in, both home and away. He put him through engineering school with no residual debt. John was more than a father to Jack. He was his best friend and trusted life coach, helping him navigate his way through good times and bad, standing by him no matter what.

Jack had just talked to him yesterday, one of two calls a week that was their pattern. Now he was gone. He couldn't believe it. He couldn't accept it. It's like he'd lost both legs or both arms.

In the blink of an eye, he walked over to the credenza on the other side of the room and drank two fingers of a single malt whiskey he kept in his office, just in case. It went down with a flip of his wrist. It had been six months since he last promised his wife he'd never have another drink, a record time for him in a series of such promises.

He needed to deaden the pain of the second savage loss that day. Just after lunch, he'd received notice from Human Resources by email that all upper managers were being replaced by people from the company that had bought them out. "Nothing personal," she said. "Just business." He'd been cleaning out his desk when the unwelcome call came from his mother.

Two casualties in one day called for another two fingers, this time sipped slowly to savor both the taste and the sense of warmth and tranquility it brought to him. After a third of the same, he decided not to take anything with him and walked out of his office for the last time. "To hell with them," he thought. "My replacement can dump it all out."

He drove slowly to the bar where he knew his old drinking buddies would welcome him back like a prodigal son. He stumbled into the front door of his house sometime after midnight.

Morning came too early. He stayed in bed until long after his wife took the two boys to school and went to her workplace. At least she had a place to go. He didn't. By noon, he was back in the world of sobriety for the time being and feeling the guilt of another broken promise to Marianne, who would come through the front door in five more hours. He was dreading it.

After six months that seemed like six years of tumbling down a bottomless pit, Jack landed another job, and his downward trajectory took a turn up. The new job was a couple notches below the one he'd lost, and it involved a lot of travel.

During those six months, it hadn't been easy for Jack's family. His drinking put everyone on edge, including Jack. Some days it wasn't so bad; some days the train came off the rails. If it wasn't for the new employment, Jack's life would have drifted into chaos and hopelessness. He'd stopped drinking again after a particularly pointed threat, and two weeks later the new career opportunity arrived on his doorstep. After two months of training, his boss pushed him out of the nest and sent him to Ireland, on his own.

The morning after his arrival, he was in a hotel room searching the Internet for an answer to a pressing question that lay in his mind like an angry dog on a short chain.

"Is there no safe place anywhere in this world?" he said to no one in particular, given that there was no one in the room when he said it. He had been looking at a poem written by a European pessimist from the 1930s who had witnessed the Great Depression and the advent of World War II.

> Danger ever with me,
> Danger before me and behind me,
> Danger beneath me and above me,
> Danger on my right and on my left,
> Danger when I lie down and when I sit down,
> Danger when I arise.

"Kind of the story of my life," he noted silently, without adding any details.

Indeed, Jack did have his share of troubles and danger in

the 36 years of his life. But did he have more than anyone else? He thought he did, but did he really? Which brings up an interesting thought—if a significant number of people have more troubles and danger than anyone else, what's the benchmark for the comparison?

Jack considered himself a Christian, ever since he gave his heart to the Lord when he went through a confirmation class in his church. But now he didn't know for sure whether he was or wasn't. If he had Jesus in his heart, why did it seem like so much went against him so much of the time.

His troubles had started six-and-a-half years ago, and so did his uncontrolled drinking. He lost $50,000 in a bad stock investment and could only erase it from his mind with the contents of a bottle. Bottle led to bottle, and the day he turned 30, he slipped into a debilitating depression that lasted nearly a year. Twelve refills of a powerful anti-depressant and twelve therapy sessions later, he slipped out of it. A year after that darkness turned to light, he suffered whiplash when his car was rear ended by a pickup truck with a cement mixer in its cargo bed. Ten days after his final rehab session, a robber coming out of an alley took his wallet and phone and punched him out as an exclamation point.

Jack thought that the Book of Job in the Bible should be replaced by the Book of Jack. He stopped those reflections when no restoration took place as happened with Job. And the more he wasn't restored, the more he drank, until he arrived at the dictionary definition of an alcoholic. In the last chapter of the book, Job's great troubles turned to great blessings, as God gave him back more than what he had before. Jack's many troubles of the past six years had a different ending—the loss of a promising career and the death of his father.

"Is this God's plan for my life?" he asked himself, as he read the poem for the third time. "What have I done to deserve this? Why me?" No answer was forthcoming. "Maybe God would answer me in a church," and off he went to Saint Fin Barre's Cathedral in the city he was in for a work trip.

He left his hotel at precisely 9 a.m. and took a right turn outside the front door toward St. Fin Barre's. He walked at a leisurely pace for a half-hour through streets broad and narrow until he reached the church. As he went through the front doors of the majestic Gothic Revival three-spire church, he came to a visitor's desk where he gave a stipulated donation to tour the church. He walked down the main aisle, not noticing the interior beauty of the church, as he inspected the diamond tiles on the floor. When he reached the altar, he turned right and shuffled to a small chapel hidden from the rest of the church. There he sat down in the last of seven pews and put his head in his hands. "I can't go on any longer like this, God," he lamented. "Please help me. Please stop my drinking and bring me out of the darkness I'm in. Show me Your mercy." He sat in silence, with his eyes closed, and absorbed the quiet, for that's all that there was.

The First Lesson

After ten minutes of listening to the sound of silence, Jack heard footsteps entering the chapel, distinctly those of a man. He kept his head in his hands and tried to stay in the moment of waiting for the voice of God. The footsteps stopped, and he felt the presence of a man standing next to his pew.

Jack dropped to his knees and put his head on the top of the wooden bench ahead of him, as a signal to the stranger that he didn't want to be disturbed. That didn't work, as a gentle voice said, "Hello Jack." Jack looked up when the man called his name, and saw someone who triggered no prior memory of existence.

Jack observed the physical dimensions of the man, as if he were going to fill out a report later for the civil police. He was about six feet tall and had a sturdy athletic build with broad chest. His hands were large and strong, like those of a football player. He had an oval face, a long straight nose with narrow bridge, light olive skin, and dark brown eyes set deep between a prominent forehead and high cheekbones. He had curly dark brown hair, medium cut, and a short beard neatly trimmed.

Jack was shorter by two inches and less defined in the body, like someone who perhaps played sports in the past but had lately spent too much time in bars. His face was somewhat square with a fleshy nose on the short side parked unobtrusively right in the middle. His eyes were green and his hair was black, cut short, with no facial hair.

Jack pushed himself to the back of his own bench. The stranger settled in the pew in front of him, turned around, and looked through him with eyes that penetrated like lasers into the depths of his soul.

"Though I don't know you," Jack said, "you seem to know me. Who exactly are you?"

"Manny," he answered, "and I do know you, but, as you said, you don't know me."

Jack had a perplexed look on his face. "How do you know me?"

Manny smiled. "That's not important right now. What's important is that you have a troubled soul and came into this church to find answers to your dilemma."

"How do you know I'm troubled and have a dilemma?" Jack sputtered out with a testy voice.

"I saw it on your face when you came into this church and when you walked slowly to this chapel, sat down with your head in your hands, and sighed the sigh of a man who doesn't know who he is or where he's going."

The testy voice went into a trash can. "I *am* troubled," Jack admitted.

Manny nodded his head but didn't say anything. Jack looked into his eyes and saw compassion and an invitation for him to unlock his heart and soul and show the stranger what existed in those hidden places. Somehow, in some way, without a clear-cut announcement of any kind, in the open air or in his mind, Jack felt that Manny wasn't a stranger at all but someone he had known his entire life—a confidante, the closest of friends, a person with whom he could intimately communicate in a way he couldn't with anyone else. It's hard to explain how such things happen, but they do happen in a realm that's beyond our immediate understanding.

"Do you know what's happened in my life in the last year?" Jack asked.

Manny nodded his head again but this time spoke. "Yes. You lost your job, lost your father, and are heading down a long road of alcoholism that won't end until you die, unless someone leads you down a different path. You also have a troubled marriage because you have not let your wife into your life. You treat her as an accessory. Even your children don't know you and feel you don't care about them in the least. You are in a very dangerous place, Jack. Your life is about to unravel in ways beyond your greatest fears."

The part about Jack's wife and kids and his unraveling life hit him like a slap in the face, which was Manny's intent.

"I don't know what to do any more," Jack sorrowfully stated. "I do feel like I'm drifting in a dangerous world and fear what the outcome may be. I don't know where to turn. I want to find a safe place but don't have a clue how to find it, if it even exists."

"Tell me more about the dangers you see," Manny asked.

"It's not just about what's happening to me," Jack responded. "The whole world is a dangerous place. When I listen to the news or read the paper, I'm inundated with danger on every side—hurricanes that kill 2,000 people, wildfires that wipe out whole towns, cancer and heart disease and car accidents that claim thousands of lives every year."

"That's all true," Manny acknowledged.

"On a personal level," Jack continued, "my sister has been diagnosed with breast cancer and my favorite uncle died last month of a stroke. My wife and I were hit by a large car that couldn't stop quickly enough on an icy road in December. We're lucky to be alive, and she's still in rehab. Where's the goodness of God in all this? Where's the safety?" Jack ran out of breath as he finished his litany and sat in silence.

"You see the world as all bad news, don't you, Jack?" Manny asked, "filled with turbulence, trouble, chaos, and crime. To you, life is like a fiddler playing the music of life in a windstorm." Manny paused.

"Let me ask you, do you not think there's any joy, peace, or safety on this earth? Or anything that can be defined as good? Do you not see that your wife and two boys are a blessing in your life?"

Jack looked at him with a blank stare.

"Would you like to see goodness about you instead of only trouble? Would you like to find the safest place on earth?"

"Where would that be?" Jack responded in a voice that was empty of any emotion. His voice gained a decibel of hope as he said, "Is there such a place? Could you show me where it is?"

Manny's face lit up. "Yes, there is such a place, and I can

help you find it. But it will take some work on your part to get there. Are you willing to let me guide you?"

Jack thought to himself, "What do I have to lose?" The fact is he had nothing to lose and everything to gain. But how could he agree to follow the directions of a man he'd just met thirty minutes ago? The answer lay in that realm that's beyond our immediate understanding.

There was something about Manny that he couldn't quite put his finger on. He spoke with the voice of authority and credibility. His face had an aura of understanding and compassion. The timbre and inflections of his voice resonated with strings hidden within Jack called hope and joy, the vibration of which he hadn't heard for years.

In the fourth chapter of John, Jesus said to Peter and his brother Andrew, "Come follow Me," and "they left their nets and followed Him." Later on He came upon James and his brother John in a boat with their father. When Jesus called them, "immediately they left the boat and their father and followed Him." The four of them didn't think twice. Jesus asked; they followed. It was that way with Jack responding to Manny's question.

"I think I can trust him?" Jack said to himself and answered Manny's question aloud with a voice more optimistic than his pessimistic nature would normally allow. "Yes, I'm willing to follow your guidance." Manny's face radiated joy when Jack gave him the green light.

Jack then spoke with the voice of a starving man who'd been wandering aimlessly for days and suddenly stumbles upon a restaurant giving out free food. "Where do we start?"

"With your first assignment," Manny answered.

"I want you to read the first three chapters in Genesis, Romans 8:28, 2 Corinthians 11:25-27, and Psalm 16. When you finish that assignment, we'll meet again."

Jack wrote down the Bible passages in the business notepad he carried with him wherever he went. "I didn't carry a Bible with me on this trip," which was a major understatement, given that he never carried a Bible anywhere he went.

"But I'm heading home tomorrow and will start my assignment then. When will we meet again and where? I won't be coming back to this city for several months."

"Don't worry about the when and where. I'll find you at the right time and place—in a couple of weeks or so. Listen carefully, Jack. I don't want you to just read through the Scripture I gave you. I want you to study it, meditate on it, and read it over and over until you wring out of it all that you possibly can."

With that said, Manny arose from his pew, stepped into the aisle, and walked briskly out of the church, with Jack still sitting in his pew turning over in his mind what had just taken place.

Lesson Two

Exactly two weeks later, Jack sat on a bench near a park-sized athletic field within Trinity College, on lunch break from the conference he was attending. The field looked like it could be used for a number of different purposes, such as soccer, but there were no soccer goals or any stands for spectators. A running track circled the field. The greenness of the grounds was striking, as green as an emerald. A ring of deciduous trees of several varieties, part of the nearly 500 trees on campus, circled the field some 80 feet from the track, and that's where the benches were, mahogany in color and made of sturdy hardwood.

As he thought about nothing in particular, he had the unmistakable sense that Manny was near, and within seconds he heard the same footsteps he had heard in Saint Fin Barre's Cathedral two weeks prior. They came from the asphalt path behind him. In the time it took to walk thirty feet, Manny sat down on the same bench, six feet from him. He was wearing a dark blue suit, white shirt, no tie. Jack had on a similar outfit, except his suit was a light brown.

"You look better today, Jack, than the last time we met," Manny announced to initiate the conversation. He wasn't referring to what Jack was wearing; he meant the expression on his face and the bearing of his demeanor.

Jack took that as a compliment. "I feel better than the last time we met. The assignment you gave me has had me thinking in a way I haven't for many years."

"In what way?" Manny asked.

"In the first chapter of Genesis, God used the word "good" six times and "very good" a seventh time, when He created Adam and Eve. I've been seeing all the bad and all the danger in the world, but that doesn't seem to be the way God created it. The second chapter describes the beauty and goodness of the Garden of Eden and God talking with Adam. It ends with the creation of Eve. Oh, how I wish I could have lived in that garden! There was no danger in it."

"That was the original safest place on earth," Manny added. "What else did you learn?"

Jack hesitated for two blinks of an eye before answering. "I had trouble with the third chapter of Genesis. Adam and Eve lost everything when Eve ate of the forbidden fruit and gave some to Adam to eat. With that one disobedience, they were thrown out of the Garden of Eden and God cursed everything in sight. I peeked ahead to the next four chapters, where Cain murders Abel and things got so bad on earth that God sent a flood to wipe out all mankind except Noah and his family.

"You've got to explain that to me. Why did one mistake doom mankind and make God so mad that he wanted to wipe out his creation with a flood. What happened to the safety and the good? And in Romans 8:28 ...."

"Hold it Jack. Let's deal with the third chapter of Genesis first before we move on to Romans and the rest of your assigned reading. If you don't understand Genesis, you'll have a problem understanding the rest of Scripture, including why Jesus came to earth and what He accomplished with His crucifixion and resurrection. I want you to just listen for the next 15 minutes, but if you have a burning question, you can ask me."

Jack sat forward, with his business notebook ready and Cross pen in hand, prepared to take notes. "I'm listening."

Manny started the lesson. "In the beginning, God created the safest place on earth. It was called the Garden of Eden, also known as Paradise. Adam was the first human created and thus the forefather of all mankind, including everyone walking the earth today. He is our natural father and Eve is our natural mother. They were commanded to be fruitful and multiply and fill the earth with people—men and women who looked like them and whose inner selves were like their inner selves.

"Because they had two eyes, two ears, and two lungs,

we have two eyes, two ears, and two lungs. Because they had one nose, one mouth, and one heart, we have one nose, one mouth, and one heart. Their inner selves, what we call their souls, were connected to God through their spirits, and our inner selves, our souls, would have also been connected to God through our spirits, except for the tragic choice Adam and Eve made in the third chapter.

"Adam represented the entire human race, and that meant that when he chose to sin, all humanity suffered the consequences. The result of turning away from our Creator was separation from Him—both in time here on earth, as physical bodies decay and die, and for eternity.

"Their spirits were alive and in tune with God's Spirit, and our spirits would have also been alive and in tune with God's Spirit, had it not been for their life-changing choice to reject God and His goodness. When they fell away from God, their spirits became dead, and that's the way we're all born into this world—having dead spirits separated from God's presence.

"Adam and Eve were the original pattern for all humanity. They were the first chapter in the history of men and women born of natural descent. If you were to trace your family line all the way back to the beginning, you'd end up with Adam as your father and Eve as your mother.

"In the midst of the Garden were the tree of life and the tree of the knowledge of good and evil—so called because good would be known if they obeyed God, and evil would be known if they disobeyed Him."

Manny pulled out a Bible from the briefcase he was carrying, opened it up to Genesis 2:8-9, and read.

> Now the LORD God had planted a garden in the east, in Eden; and there he put the man he had formed. The LORD God made all kinds of trees grow out of the ground—trees that were pleasing to the eye and good for food. In the middle of the garden were the tree of life and the tree of the knowledge of good and evil.

Then he read Genesis 2:15-17.

> The LORD God took the man and put him in
> the Garden of Eden to work it and take care of it.
> And the LORD God commanded the man, "You are
> free to eat from any tree in the garden; but you must
> not eat from the tree of the knowledge of good and
> evil, for when you eat from it you will certainly die."

Followed by Genesis 2:18-22.

> The LORD God said, "It is not good for the
> man to be alone. I will make a helper suitable for
> him." ... So the LORD God caused the man to fall
> into a deep sleep; and while he was sleeping, he took
> one of the man's ribs and then closed up the place
> with flesh. Then the LORD God made a woman from
> the rib he had taken out of the man, and he brought
> her to the man.

And finally Genesis 3: 20

> Adam named his wife Eve, because she would
> become the mother of all the living.

"The description given of the garden was of a large area through which rivers flowed. It was called *Eden*, which means *Paradise*. It was located east of where Adam was created.

"Paradise was the original safest place on earth. God created it to be so. For Adam and Eve there would be no death, sickness, diseases, accidents, or disasters. They would not be trapped by addictions, fear, depression, or anxiety. You wish it would have stayed that way for all their descendants down to you. You're not the first one to wish that." How did Manny know what Jack wished for?

Jack took in a deep breath and said, "You've got that right! The first two chapters of Genesis were so hopeful, but the air came out of me with Genesis 3."

Manny continued. "We find in the 2nd and 3rd chapters of Genesis that God walked in the Garden and talked with Adam and Eve. It was an unbroken relationship that would continue on forever—as long as Adam and Eve listened to God and didn't disobey the one command He gave them.

"There was no safer place on earth than to be in Paradise and connected to God. Did you notice that I said *was?*"

"I noticed," Jack answered.

Manny pulled a small electronic tablet out of the same briefcase and showed Jack this graph. Jack wondered to himself, "So this is the original safest place on earth, with no danger of any kind."

God

Adam and Eve

"The word safest is a relative word," Manny explained. "It's not absolute." He needed to correct Jack's thinking, but how did he know what Jack was thinking? "It doesn't mean Paradise was totally safe. How could it be with Satan lurking in the shadows, just waiting to get revenge on God for throwing him—Lucifer at the time—out of heaven? Lucifer's unforgivable sin was that, in his pride, he wanted to be just like God."

Jack had been listening closely, but at that point, his mind threw up a red flag and demanded more information. "Huh? You just lost me with that matter of Lucifer and Satan. I need some background."

Manny smiled. "I thought you might. The serpent's body in Paradise had been taken over by Satan the devil, who had been Lucifer in heaven. He was a glorious angelic being whose name meant "Morning Star," which we find in Isaiah 14:12. Lucifer was the most splendid one among the angelic beings, and his beauty, exalted position, and close proximity to God's throne caused him to covet God's glory and lead a revolt to establish himself as another god. Other angels in heaven joined him in a revolt against God." At that point, Manny opened his Bible to Ezekiel 28:17.

> "Your heart became proud on account of your beauty, and you corrupted your wisdom because of your splendor."

"In all his pride and defiance, he became Satan the devil. Satan means adversary, and devil means slanderer. Isaiah 14:12-15 tells of his fall from his lofty position.

> How have you fallen from heaven, O morning star, son of the dawn! You have been cast down to the earth, you who once laid low the nations! You said in your heart, "I will ascend to heaven; I will raise my throne above the stars of God; I will sit enthroned on the mount of assembly, on the utmost height of the sacred mountain. I will ascend above the tops of the clouds. I will make myself like the Most High." But you are brought down to the grave, to the depths of the pit.

"Lucifer, the glorious angelic being, became Satan the devil and was cast out of his position in heaven to the lower place of earth and drew a third of the angels with him, as we find in Revelation 12:4. Ephesians 2:2 says he became 'the ruler of the air, the spirit who is now at work in those who are disobedient.' He stands as prince of the organized kingdom of darkness opposed to the kingdom of light. This will be his realm until the time of the end when Michael the archangel will cast him and his angels down during the tribulation period.

"So, you see, Satan tempted God's human creation; thus, sin had its beginning in the heart of an angel.

"Now let's turn back to Adam and Eve. They were safe until they listened to the tempter. It's like a child who is safe in her own house with her parents in control, but when she walks to play at a friend's house a block away, she encounters an evil man on the street who offers her a piece of candy laced with drugs that will kill her.

"You see, Jack, mankind was created to associate and fellowship with God eternally. All Adam and Eve—and everyone who would descend from them—had to do was acknowledge that God was their loving King and Master. He was the greater, and they were the lesser. He was God, and they were not. He would take care of them if they would trust Him and be obedient to Him.

"Theirs was a world that was fruitful and without danger and safe—as long as they accepted their rightful status of letting God be above them and listening to Him and obeying His authority over them. Notice I said *was*. But then something happened, and this world was no longer perfectly safe. Danger was introduced into God's creation, not by His will but by their disobedience. And there was no going back to the safest place on earth—ever!"

Manny's words flowed into Jack like precious oil poured into an earthen vessel. He just wanted to sit on the bench all day and listen to Manny, but his lunch hour was nearly over and the conference would resume in ten minutes.

Manny stood up and said, "You need to get back to your meetings, don't you? What time do they end today?"

"At 4 p.m.," Jack answered, as he got up to head back.

"Then let's meet back here at exactly 4:15," Manny said, like a captain giving orders to his troops. "We need to complete the lesson of Genesis 3 today."

There was no need for Jack to say anything. The time was set. The class would continue.

Lesson Three

The Holy Spirit filled Jack's mind with Genesis during the afternoon conference sessions, without blocking out his awareness of the medical equipment presentations. It was like a juggler keeping two balls in the air at the same time.

When the last session ended fifteen minutes early, Jack was able to touch base with his boss before returning to the athletic field. They agreed to meet for supper and review the information received that day and discuss what impact it might have on their company.

Jack approached the same athletic field bench, beside a magnificent Ginkgo Biloba tree. Manny was already there, reading his Bible, his electronic tablet beside him.

"How did your meetings go?" Manny asked before Jack sat down. Jack sensed that Manny really wanted to know how the meetings went and was not just making small talk.

"It was, how can I say it, (Jack paused) peculiar. I was able to meditate on our noon Bible lesson and The Future of Class 3 Medical Devices in Western Europe at the same time. Maybe remarkable is a better word."

"Hmm," Manny replied, "who would have thought that possible?" he added with a smile that slanted to one side.

"I'm meeting for dinner with the CEO of my company at 6:30, so we have at least an hour to finish the Genesis lesson. Will that be enough time?"

Manny motioned for Jack to sit down on the bench. "That will be more than enough time. Our lessons are like teaching and learning in a college classroom. It's hard for students to take in much more than an hour. Shall we start?"

Jack made himself comfortable on the bench and nodded his head. "I'm ready."

Manny turned toward Jack and started the lesson. "Over the noon hour, I told you something happened in Paradise that brought danger into God's creation. Do you remember that?"

"That's what I was thinking about all afternoon," Jack answered. "You know how concerned I am about danger. I've been racking my brains to figure it out and can't get beyond Adam and Eve and the forbidden fruit. I've always blamed God for giving us such a broken world, but I think you're going to paint a different picture."

"Oh, you mustn't blame God," Manny declared with a tone of uneasiness. "Listen closely to me, and you will receive the most important insight of your life—up to this day. Your distorted view of God's working in this world needs to be removed, in a similar manner to dredging sludge and debris from a waterway. Your misinformation has caused you to live in a pattern of doubt, distrust, and anxiety. Until you know and understand what really happened in the third chapter of Genesis, you'll continue to fight your way through a thick dark fog of your own thinking. You need to change your paradigm of God and His creation to find safety in this dangerous world.

Jack raised his hand to ask a question, like a student in a classroom. "I know what a paradigm is in the medical field—the basic assumptions shared by a scientific community—but what do *you* mean by that word, so we're on the same page."

"Let's make it simple," Manny answered. "It's how you see the world, which for you is filled with danger and pain everywhere and God's seeming indifference to all the bad things happening in His creation. I don't mean to make you feel bad, but the word that best describes your spiritual paradigm is ignorance."

Being called ignorant is one thing, stating that a person has ignorance in a particular subject matter is quite another. Jack took Manny's assessment well.

"I don't think that's a hard word at all to describe my understanding of what happened in the third chapter of Genesis. In fact, it's a accurate word. Since the antidote to ignorance is knowledge, I hope that's where we're heading now."

Manny smiled and his eyes twinkled with joy. Some people are apt students; many are not. Of course, he already knew Jack would fit into the wanting-to-learn student mold. "That's indeed where we're heading now.

"What really happened back then? Adam and Eve didn't put their faith in God or trust Him or obey Him. They were like the child I told you about who didn't listen to her parents when they told her not to take anything from strangers. The little girl took the deadly candy because the desire to enjoy sweetness was greater than the warning from her parents, and when she ate of it she died. In a similar way, Adam and Eve fell for Satan's lie that they could be like God Himself if they ate the fruit from the Tree of the Knowledge of Good and Evil. The result of their disobedience is called The Fall, and it takes place in the 3rd chapter of Genesis in the Bible." Manny opened his Bible and read verses 1-5.

> Now the serpent was more crafty than any of the wild animals the LORD God had made. He said to the woman, "Did God really say, 'You must not eat from any tree in the garden'?"
> The woman said to the serpent, "We may eat fruit from the trees in the garden, but God did say, 'You must not eat fruit from the tree that is in the middle of the garden, and you must not touch it, or you will die.'"
> "You will not certainly die," the serpent said to the woman. "For God knows that when you eat from it your eyes will be opened, and you will be like God, knowing good and evil."

"Satan didn't introduce temptation as rebellion against God. He proposed it as an opportunity to obtain something presumably good outside of God's provision. And that's the way it is today. People don't say, 'I'm an evil person, and I'm going to do bad things.' They fall into it gradually. It's what C.S. Lewis said about the path to hell: 'The safest road to hell is the gradual one—the gentle slope, soft underfoot, without sudden turnings, without milestones, without signposts.' For people who fall into drug addiction, it starts with the first sampling of the forbidden meth or cocaine, for example, just to try it out because others are using it or to see what a high feels like. That's what Eve did with the forbidden fruit." Manny read verse 6.

> When the woman saw that the fruit of the
> tree was good for food and pleasing to the eye, and
> also desirable for gaining wisdom, she took some
> and ate it.
> She also gave some to her husband, who was
> with her, and he ate it.

"When Eve gave the forbidden fruit to Adam to eat, the whole of creation fell from a very safe place to a very dangerous place. That's the world we live in today—a world of death, disease, and destruction. They exchanged the right to be obedient to a loving God for their own rights in defiance of God. They, in effect, separated themselves from God, and the depths of mankind's being became disoriented by sin.

"The result is seen on every page of the Bible after the 3rd chapter of Genesis. Beyond the Bible, the result is evident in recorded world history down to the present day, on the front pages of newspapers, on TV and radio broadcasts, in social media postings, in court records and jail and prison bookings, and in the behavior of your neighbor down the street."

Manny picked up the tablet on the bench and showed Jack this graphic.

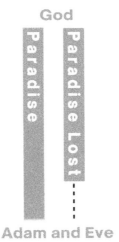

"The first bar represents the original safest place on earth—God's creation as He meant it to be, men and women connected to God. When Adam and Eve sinned, they became separated from God. The second bar represents the fallen world they bequeathed to us—knowing good and evil but no longer connected to God in a relationship of trust and obedience.

"Now what? The precedent had already been set. God threw Lucifer and the unfaithful and rebellious fallen angels out of heaven. And that's exactly what he did with Adam and Eve. He threw them out of Paradise to wander in a dangerous spiritual wasteland.

"Then came the ultimate blow. He cursed the fallen and sinful world in which they chose to live. That curse is recorded in Genesis 3:17-19.

> To Adam he said, "Because you listened to
> your wife and ate fruit from the tree about which I
> commanded you, 'You must not eat from it,'
> > "Cursed is the ground because of you;
> > > through painful toil you will eat food from it
> > > all the days of your life.
> > It will produce thorns and thistles for you,
> > > and you will eat the plants of the field.
> > By the sweat of your brow
> > > you will eat your food
> > until you return to the ground,
> > > since from it you were taken;
> > for dust you are
> > > and to dust you will return."

"We also find mention of the curse in Isaiah 24:6. Manny turned to that verse and read.

> Therefore a curse consumes the earth; its
> people must bear their guilt.

"And the curse is echoed in Malachi 2:1-2 for priests who do not honor God, which was the sin of Adam and Eve.

> "And now, you priests, this warning is for you.
> If you do not listen, and if you do not resolve to honor

my name," says the LORD Almighty, "I will send a curse on you, and I will curse your blessings. Yes, I have already cursed them, because you have not resolved to honor me."

"Take a look at the world we live in today, Jack. Sin and evil are everywhere. Men and women are attracted to evil, are involved in it, and some even delight with a sense of accomplishment in their sinful ways. Let's look at Romans 5:12.

> Therefore, just as sin entered the world
> through one man, and death through sin, and in this
> way death came to all people, because all sinned.

"So you see, my friend, you have been suffering from an acute case of ignorance and misunderstanding. You think, 'Why would a good God allow such bad things to happen in this world? Things like earthquakes, floods, and wildfires, and horrible things like the holocaust, pandemics, mental illness, and children languishing in cancer wards. There are bad people doing awful things to good people. Where is God in all this?'"

Manny surprised Jack by listing the very things that Jack would have listed if Manny had asked him for such an inventory two weeks ago. "That's exactly what I think, Manny, or at least used to think."

Manny stood up and continued with the dramatic flair of a street preacher cautioning a crowd on a corner.

"We live in a world where drugs and alcohol get the best of many people and where crime, cancer, and catastrophes are everyday occurrences. Who's to blame for all this? 'It can't be us,' cry the uninformed. 'It must be God's fault, if there even is a God. A good God would never allow such awful things to happen.' That's what people think who are not familiar with the Bible."

Jack slumped over, put his head down, and raised his hand, as if to say, "That's me, Manny. I'm ashamed of myself." But he didn't say anything out loud.

Manny continued. "You don't have to be ashamed, Jack. You've now reached the point of being an awakened spirit. You are eager to learn what is really spiritually true, not what you think is true.

"Truth comes from God, not man. The way we are is not God's design. It never was. He gave goodness and grace to Adam and Eve and all their descendants. In the beginning, there would be no death, no sickness, no catastrophes, and no bad things happening at any time. It would be the safest place on earth. But Adam and Eve, our original parents, said, 'No thanks. We'd rather go our own way and be our own gods, if You don't mind.' But God did mind; He minded very much.

"Adam and Eve stepped away from a safe and perfect world when they chose their way over God's way, when they wanted to know themselves apart from God. And they imparted to us a sinful disposition and a world that is as dangerous as it once was safe.

"In this fallen and cursed world, anything is possible. Only through the grace and mercy of God does the world not fall into total chaos.

"Satan had said, 'You will not certainly die.' In a way that was true. Adam and Eve didn't immediately die physically. They still had a body and a soul. But their spiritual life became desert-like dry. The intimate connection they had with God through their spirits became a vast wasteland. As their descendants, all people are born into that dangerous wasteland, which is why they need salvation. It's why you need salvation, Jack."

With that last exhortation, Manny, the street preacher, sat back down on the bench. He didn't look at the clock on the scoreboard at the far end of the athletic field, but he knew that an hour had been reached. He could also tell that Jack had about as much teaching as he could absorb in one sitting.

"Do you think you're saved, Jack?" Manny asked out of the blue. "Do you really believe you've been born-again, and how did that happen?"

Jack was surprised at the question. He thought that Manny assumed he was a Christian, but given the information of the past hour, he wasn't sure he really was. Jack's world had been turned upside down, and he didn't even know what being saved actually meant or who a true Christian was.

He felt sheepish when he related how he had been saved. "At the last meeting of our confirmation class, the associate pastor asked us if we accepted Jesus as our Savior. He told us we couldn't be confirmed unless we were saved. We all raised our hands except one girl, and she was confirmed with the rest of us the following Sunday anyway. What do you think, Manny, was I saved then or not?"

Manny had been listening closely and compassionately. "It's not up to me to say whether you were saved then or not. You first need to get a firm grasp on what being saved really means, which is also known as being born-again or reborn."

Jack glanced at his watch. "Do we have time to do that now?"

Manny shook his head back and forth. "No, that will need to be the subject of another hour. Besides, you need to digest what we've just covered and to think about it and to pray on the verses I read to you today. Take time tonight after your dinner with Michael; we'll talk again tomorrow."

Jack couldn't remember telling Manny that his boss's name was Michael. But maybe he did; otherwise, how would he know?

"The conference finishes up at noon tomorrow," Jack said, "and then I head back to the States."

"Is Michael flying back with you?"

"Yes. He has a limousine picking us up at the hotel at 1 p.m. to take us to the airport, and we'll be together in the airport until we fly out at 4;30. I don't see a window for us to meet."

Manny stood up and said, "It'll work out. Do your study tonight, and I'll see you tomorrow." Then he turned and walked off toward the east entrance of the college.

Lesson Four

During breakfast the next morning, before the conference's first session, Michael told Jack there was a change of
plans for him. He found out after dinner the night before that a
hospital administrator in London wanted to talk to him about
a possible sale of high-frequency ventilators. A lot of money
was on the table, so he arranged a short flight the next day for
a mid-morning meeting. It was so close, he said, that it didn't
make sense to return to the States and then fly back to London. Michael said that he'd already booked the limousine, so
Jack could ride in comfort to the airport all by himself. Kind-
ness and generosity were two traits Michael had in abundant
supply.

The conference ended at noon. Jack walked the block
back to his hotel, packed up, and was in the lobby at 12:50 to
await his ride to the airport. At exactly 1 p.m., the limo pulled
up and the driver put Jack's bags in the trunk and opened the
back door for Jack to enter a space that had a horseshoe-shaped
ring of seats that started at the door he entered and ended at
the door on the other side. There was enough room for eight
passengers.

"Lots a traffic," the driver announced in a heavy Irish
brogue, as he started to close the door. "I tink it'll take us a
good hour to get to the aerfort from here." Jack nodded his
head. No sense in saying anything. He'd still get there in time
even if it took an hour and a half.

As his door closed, the door on the other side of the limo
opened, and in stepped Manny. Jack was knocked for a loop
and couldn't catch his breath to say anything. His face must
have told Manny all he needed to know.

"You told me a limousine would be picking you up at

1 p.m.," Manny said.

Jack finally caught his breath. "But I also told you Michael would be with me."

"That you did," Manny laughed, "but I see Michael isn't here."

"That's because his plans changed, and he's going to London tomorrow instead. But you knew that, didn't you? How did you know?"

Manny shrugged his shoulders. "We have much to cover in the hour to the airport. We'd best get started." Not only did Manny know that Jack would be traveling by himself, but he also knew that it would take an hour to get to the airport for a trip that normally took a half hour.

Manny had the serious look that a captain of a company of soldiers would have when ordering them into a major battle. "Today could very well be the most important day of your life. Today, you'll find out whether you're saved or not."

"I barely slept last night," Jack responded, "thinking about that. First off, I need to know what it means to be born-again or saved or born of the Spirit or any of the other terminology I've heard in religious circles. I just assumed it had all been taken care of during my confirmation, when I raised my hand to accept Jesus into my heart."

"Maybe it was taken care of then and maybe it wasn't. We'll soon find out. Let's start with an outline of what it means to be a real Christian—that is, a believer and a Christ follower. Those are two more terms that mean basically the same thing."

Manny sat opposite Jack in the limo instead of alongside him, as with the previous three meetings. There was a sound-proof divider between the driver and the passengers, so they had a meeting area all to themselves. Manny started the lesson.

"The fall of Adam and Eve, God's curse on the earth, and their being ushered out of Paradise would have been the end of the story for all mankind—separated from God forever with a one-way ticket to eternal damnation. But John 3:16 tells us that's not what a loving God wanted then or wants today. He wants all of us to come back into the relationship with Him that Adam and Eve had in the beginning.

> For God so loved the world that He gave His
> One and only Son, that whoever believes in Him shall
> not perish but have everlasting life.

We saw in Genesis 3:17-19 that God cursed the earth, and we are all born into a fallen world. But to the problem of sin and separation, God had a solution—the promise of a Messiah, a Savior, to restore and reconnect us to Himself, as it was in the beginning in Eden. I see you have your Bible with you. Open it up and read Genesis 3:15. That verse should be lit up in neon lights, with trumpets blaring and bells ringing. And why don't you read the verse before it as well."

Jack turned to those verses and read.

> So the LORD God said to the serpent, "Be-
> cause you have done this,
> > "Cursed are you above all livestock
> > and all wild animals!
> > You will crawl on your belly
> > and you will eat dust
> > all the days of your life.

"That's verse 14," Jack said. "Now I'll read the 15th verse with a simulation of trumpets blaring and bells ringing." He used his best thespian voice and projected those 27 words as if he were talking to someone 40 feet away.

> **"And I will put enmity**
> > **between you and the woman,**
> > **and between your offspring and hers;**
> **he will crush your head,**
> > **and you will strike his heel."**

Manny took over. "The serpent is Satan, who in the end will be thrown into a lake of burning sulfur in the Book of Revelation. The woman is Eve, whose offspring will lead to Jesus Christ. Christ's heel will be struck when He dies on the cross, but He will crush the head of Satan and redeem mankind from the curse with His resurrection. The death sentence of eternal separation from God that resulted with the fall is rendered null and void by being born-again from the spirit of the natural world into the Spirit of God—which is salvation.

It occurs when we vacate our allegiance to the sovereignty of ourselves and the natural world and accept the Spirit of God to come live in us. We are saved *from* the curse and saved *into* an intimate relationship with God, as it was in Paradise."

Manny shifted gears like a race car driver coming into a sharp curve. "Speaking of salvation, how does someone become saved or born-again anyway? By the way, both words mean the same thing.

Jack understood that to be a rhetorical question and remained silent. Manny continued. "By doing more good than bad or belonging to a church? Repeating just the right words or following some ritual? Can people be saved by growing up in a Christian home? Let's see what the Bible has to say."

Manny turned to Ephesians 2:8-9 and read. Then did a quick flip to Titus 3:5 for a following verse.

> For it is by grace you have been saved, through faith—and this is not from yourselves, it is the gift of God—not by works, so that no one can boast.

> He saved us, not because of righteous things we had done, but because of his mercy. He saved us through the washing of rebirth and renewal by the Holy Spirit.

"We don't deserve saving, and we can't save ourselves, any more than the Apostle Paul could save anyone or a church pastor or a saintly person down the street. Salvation comes from God's mercy and grace given to those who approach Him with a seeking heart, who want to die to their natural sinful state and be born-again into a new spiritual connection to God forever.

Manny took his electronic tablet from his briefcase and showed the graphic on the next page to Jack, while saying, "Let's add two more pieces to the drawings we've already looked at."

He handed the tablet over to Jack, who cradled it in both hands and looked at the drawing with great interest.

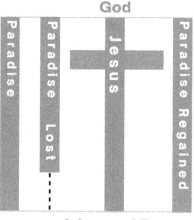

"It's the crucifixion and death of Jesus Christ that makes us right with God. Jesus took the curse upon himself on the cross and imparted His holiness and sinlessness into us to make us acceptable to God. Our sins are taken away, yes, but more importantly we are made right with our Creator. We switch our allegiance—from ourselves and the world and Satan's lies—to Him and His goodness and grace for us. World here means the natural unredeemed world, under the curse.

"If that were the end of the story, everyone would be saved. To be born-again, to move from the second column to the fourth column, we need to come to the cross and accept His sacrifice for our sins. It's God's triumph through Jesus Christ that reconciles us to Himself, and we regain what was lost in Paradise after the disobedience and pride of Adam and Eve."

Jack had a puzzled look on his face, as if he had been given a calculus formula to solve and had never studied calculus.

"What's meant by this accepting thing?" he asked. "Is it something we think in our minds or say with our lips or raise our hands in a confirmation class? If that's the case, then I must be saved."

Manny's eyebrows pinched together and his eyes penetrated into Jack's very being. "No. That's not it at all. Let's say someone has a suitcase filled with a million dollars. And the person says, 'This suitcase is all yours. Have a nice rest of your life.' Would that make you rich? No. You'd only become worth a million if you reached out and took the suitcase into your own hands. There needs to be an exchange, Jack. Jesus' death on the cross doesn't do you any good unless you receive it by your own choice—that is, you exchange your natural life for His life.

"Look at the drawing in the tablet. We're all born into the Paradise Lost position because we're descended from Adam and Eve. And there we stay, separated from God here on earth and for all eternity, unless we say, in some fashion or another, 'I'd like another choice, please. I'm not content with where I am. I want to leave my sinful life and become a child of God.'

"The Bible tells you about the critical choice you have to make. You can choose Paradise Regained in the chart if you receive Jesus' sacrifice on the cross to free you from the curse and give you the gift of eternal life in heaven. In short, you turn away from your old natural self and turn toward a regained relationship with Jesus Christ and His Father, through the power of the Holy Spirit. Everyone is first born into a natural self. Those who choose Jesus become re-born into a spiritual self, and that makes all the difference. They cross over from spiritual death to Spiritual life." He pulled another Bible out of his briefcase; this one the Amplified Bible, and he read 2 Corinthians 5:17.

> Therefore if anyone is in Christ [that is, grafted in, joined to Him by faith in Him as Savior], he is a new creature [reborn and renewed by the Holy Spirit]; the old things [the previous moral and spiritual condition] have passed away. Behold, new things have come [because spiritual awakening brings a new life].

Manny was on a roll. "Sounds good, you might say, but how does this come about? Is there a ritual to follow? Secret words? Being baptized as an infant? No, no, and no. It's a God thing, not a you thing. God knows what's in your heart; you can't fool Him or fake it. Some people are saved in an instant, others over a period of time. It's as simple as A B C.

"I can't tell you whether you're saved or not, Jack, because I don't know what was in your heart when you raised your hand to accept Jesus as your Savior so many years back. My suggestion is to go through the ABCs right now to make sure. If you're already saved, this will be renewing your vows, so to speak. If you weren't saved back then, you can make sure you are now. How does that sound?"

Jack was leaning forward on his seat and spoke quickly. "That sounds perfect," he said. "I want to make sure." He had the expectation of a top-ten professional golfer who had a two-inch putt to win the Masters.

"Let's start with the A, Jack. It stands for Admit. Do you Admit you are a sinner from birth, being the offspring of Adam and Eve, and with so many sins of your own?"

"That's an easy one," Jack said. "I Admit I'm a sinner through and through. The Bible verses you've shared with me tell the story that I've inherited a sinful nature, and my life is evidence that I've gone the extra mile with all my own sins."

"You have it absolutely right, Jack," Manny said. "Let's move to the B. It stands for Believe. Do you Believe what Jesus Christ said about Himself in John 14:6."

> I am the way and the truth and the life. No
> one comes to the Father except through me.

"That's what we talked about yesterday and on this trip to the airport, Manny. You taught me that's what the Bible's all about. I believe it in my heart, like I believe the sun's going to rise tomorrow morning. I guess I must be born-again, right, cause I believed that way back when? Oops, we have a C left, don't we?"

"Yes we do, Jack. It's the most important step because it's an act of your will. Admitting and Believing are necessary, for sure. But if you don't Choose to accept His death for your sins and turn your life over to Him, you just have head knowledge. You'd have an awakened soul but not a born-again spirit.

"In other words, Jack, you Choose His way instead of the way of Adam, the world, yourself, and the tempter, who is Satan."

Jack's head was bowed. Manny didn't need to tell him what to do next. The Holy Spirit did. His voice was charged with sincerity and solemness, as if he were applying for citizenship in a new country.

"Lord Jesus, I admit I was born with a sinful nature like the Bible says and I've committed more sins than I can remember." Jack paused to collect his thoughts. "I can see now that I've been going my own way from the day I was born and doing my own thing. If there's anyone that needs saving from a sinful life, it's me."

Jack stopped and drew in a deep breath of air, as if he were about to be immersed in water. "The Bible says You're the way, the truth, and the life and no one can be saved without Your crucifixion. I don't fully understand all of this dying on the cross for my sins stuff, but something inside me tells me it's true. I believe with all my heart that You gave Your life for me to save me." Jack paused to wipe the tears from his eyes. "You must really love me, Jesus, and I love You for what you did for me. "

Jack took another deep breath, as if he were about to make the most important decision of his life, which in fact he was.

"Right here and right now, Lord Jesus, I choose Your way instead of my way. I want to follow You until the day I die. I've been going the wrong way, and now I want to go the right way —Your way. What all that means for me, I don't know now, but I guess You'll show me, right?" Jack's mind searched for what else he could say, but nothing showed up. He summed up what he'd already said, to put a period at the end of his confession of faith so to speak. "I choose You as my Savior with all my will right now and as the Lord of my life from this day on. Amen."

There were no flashing lights or trumpets blaring. Jack didn't jump up and yell, "Hallelujah." But he knew in his heart that he had been born-again and that his life would never be the same again.

Manny clapped his hands, as if he were at a graduation ceremony, and spoke with the joy of a proud father. "Now you know for sure, Jack. You are as saved as saved can be. I'll be very interested in how this plays out in your life, starting with today and continuing on when you get back to the States."

Just then, the limo pulled up to the Aer Lingus door and Manny got out onto the sidewalk and walked slowly away. Jack wanted to stay in the limo and bask in his salvation, but the driver opened the door for him, and his luggage was at his feet.

The Next Two Years

The next 18 months for Jack were spent living out 2 Corinthians 5:17, as written in the dusty Bible he'd pulled off his bookshelf after meeting with Manny the first time.

> Therefore if anyone is in Christ, he is a new
> creation; the old has gone, the new has come.

The changes within his family exceeded the sum total of all that was good since the day he married Marianne. In the second meeting at the athletic field in Trinity College, Manny had asked Jack if he loved his wife and children. Jack answered that of course he did. Manny then asked him to define love, and Jack mumbled and stumbled and searched his mind desperately, like a librarian looking for a valuable book in a forgotten storage room.

He found something amidst the cobwebs in the storage room and shared it with Manny. "Love is a feeling of affection for someone. It's, um, a feeling of connection, you know, like really liking someone and wanting to be with them and sharing things with them." He could see Manny wasn't impressed.

Then he took an elevator down to the basement of his mind and found something he'd memorized in his confirmation class, taken from the book of Corinthians he thought. He dealt it to Manny, like someone passing off an ace from the bottom of the deck. "I remember a definition of love in the Bible," thinking that would be more profound. "Love is patient and kind. It doesn't boast or be proud. It doesn't dishonor others. It keeps no record of wrongs and rejoices in truth and goodness." He didn't have it quite right, but it was close.

Jack looked at Manny after his recitation and saw that his eyebrows were pinched again and his eyes were squinting and a deep frown was etched in his forehead. That wasn't a good sign.

"Those are attributes of love, Jack," Manny said quietly. "I asked you for a definition."

With a voice somewhere between annoyance and uneasiness, he answered Manny, "Then I don't know. I don't know what you want!"

Manny's voice softened. "Then I'll give you a working definition you can use to gauge whether you really love someone or not. *Love is doing what's best for the other person.* When you do what is best for Marianne and your two boys, then you'll be showing them love."

On the long flight back to the States, Jack knew he wanted to show love to his family like he never had before. He realized how selfish he'd been, and wanted to be a new person with them. The definition of love Manny gave him flashed in his mind like a neon billboard. "I'll do what's best for them," he said to himself. "I will, I will, I will!"

And he did. Marianne was a believer, but lonely in her faith because she could not share it with Jack or have an open Christian fellowship as a family. The two boys were growing up in a house with divided allegiance.

That all changed when Jack flew back home after a flight transfer in Chicago. He had a long talk with Marianne about what happened to him at Trinity College and on the way to the airport. She was overjoyed that there was now a man of faith in the family. At least he said he was, and he had never done that before. She gave him the benefit of the doubt because a stated relationship with Christ and the way it came about rang true. The boys didn't need an explanation; they needed his time and attention, and he gave it to them. For the first time, they had a father who loved them.

The whole family went to church every Sunday and were involved in its activities during the week. Jack got up an hour early every morning for prayer and worship and Scripture reading and meditation. He longed to get as close to Jesus as he could get. It's where Manny had told him was the safest place on earth.

His friendships became richer as his former shallowness became deeper. He joined a men's Bible study Saturday mornings and, as anyone could see, he was a man who was in love with the Lover of his soul. He put in the time after his life had changed on a dime.

And then, six months after the one-year anniversary of his salvation, he came down from the mountaintop into the valley, where everyday life distracted him from dedication to his spiritual growth and passionate-for-Christ life. He drifted. He lost his focus. His company went through a merger, and he was putting in 12-hour days, or more. The morning worship time got lost in the shuffle. He still put in the time with his wife and two boys, but it was more out of duty than out of love. He even started drinking again, not as much as before, but more than enough to make a difference in all his relationships, including that with God the Father and His Son, Jesus Christ.

For the next six months, up to the second anniversary of his being born-again, Jack was on a spiritual slope heading steadily downward. Each day he was further from God than the day before. One bad week followed another. When measured by months, it was like watching a person with inoperable cancer wasting away until becoming only a shadow of a previously healthy self. Jack was a Christian shadow, hardly recognizable as someone who had given his life to Christ.

As it happens with spiritual waste-aways, the more he drifted, the less he recognized it. He needed a wake-up call, and Marianne and the pastor of his church gave it to him. They met on a Saturday morning, which worked for Jack because he was no longer going to his Bible study. Marianne started out by saying how much she loved Jack and how much she was concerned that he was losing his way. The pastor said more of the same.

Jack listened for half an hour without saying a word. What he heard was painful. What he received in his soul was truth, and he recognized it for what it was. "I don't know what to say," he whispered when they were finished. He was slumped on a couch in the prayer room. "I didn't realize I had fallen that far."

The pastor looked at Jack. "Do you believe what we've told you about yourself?"

Jack was now perched on the front edge of the couch. "I do. It's hard to hear, but I see it clearly. I am who you say I am. I'm so ashamed and sorry. I've become who I never wanted to be again. I don't know what else to say."

The pastor spoke words of comfort. "You don't have to say anything other than what you just said. Our intent was to bring you to an awareness of how far you'd slipped. That's now been accomplished." At that point the pastor got up out of his chair and laid his hands on Jack's shoulder. Marianne got up at the same time and put her hands on his other shoulder. It seemed as if they had rehearsed it.

"Oh, Lord," the pastor prayed, "bring this wandering sheep back into your flock. Put people in his life to encourage him to walk in Your ways and to stay close to You."

Marianne prayed, "Heavenly Father, I beg you to change my husband back to who he was—a lover of Your Son, the husband I've always wanted, and the loving father our boys have come to respect. In Jesus' name."

When the laying on of hands and fervent prayers were concluded, Jack humbly arose and took Marianne's hand and walked out of the church to their car and then home.

The next morning, Jack was back in the lower level of their home, an hour before anyone else was up. "Lord, I can't do this on my own," he prayed. "I need help. Please guide me in the way I should go. Please show me why I slipped and how to make sure I never go that way again. Quicken the Holy Spirit within me to be the captain of my ship. I've proven I can't sail it with my own wind."

Two days later, Jack was on a flight to meet with his company's largest client, the University of Chicago Medical Center. His company paid for him to fly first class, one of the perks of being the top sales engineer during the last year. He had chosen an aisle seat, hoping no one would pick the remaining seat to the left of him. Ten minutes before the take-off time, he heard footsteps coming up behind him. "It can't be," he thought, with a heightened awareness and an anticipation in his spirit, not unlike a person answering the front door to see TV cameras and a woman holding a check for the Reader's Digest grand prize.

"Good morning, Jack," Manny said, as he slipped into the seat by the window. "Do you mind if I fly with you to Chicago?"

"Did you know how much I needed you right now?" Jack answered. He paused briefly. "Of course you did. Why am I not surprised?"

Manny laughed as if Jack had told him the funniest joke in the world. "Of course I did," he agreed. "Let's get down to business. We have an hour and a half before we land in Chicago."

Lesson Five

"You've been wondering how you can be a born-again Christian—redeemed from your sinful nature and having all your sins forgiven—and then fall back into the worldly, do-it-my-own-way alcoholic you were before your salvation on the way to the Dublin airport. You feared you'd lost your salvation when your wife and Pastor Dan confronted you in the prayer room. You've repented of your backsliding but aren't sure God will take you back after your rejecting Him with such abandon. And now you don't know what to do or where to go or how to restore what you had for the first year and a half after your salvation, before the bottom fell out."

Once again, Manny knew exactly what Jack had been thinking and feeling.

"You've stated my fears and anxiety as if you've been reading my mind," Jack said, no longer surprised that Manny knew all about him. "Why did my undoing happen? I thought I was safe, and now I'm right back in the dangerous world I'd left behind. How can this be? I thought God had my back. I've read His promise to me in 2 Timothy 4:18 over and over and over again, but it hasn't been true in my life." He started to open his Bible to that verse, but Manny recited it from memory.

> The Lord will rescue me from every evil attack
> and will bring me safely to his heavenly kingdom.
> To him be glory for ever and ever. Amen.

Manny was kind in his response, like a mother who wants to straighten out the thinking of her foolish son, but without accusation. "God's promises are always true, Jack. You feel that God has moved away from you, but that's not the case at all. God didn't move; you did."

Manny paused and Jack interjected, "Huh?"

"I think a picture will help you understand what I mean," Manny said. He took his electronic tablet out of the briefcase he'd brought with him on the plane and opened it to the fourth graphic, which introduced a different concept than the first three. He handed it over to Jack.

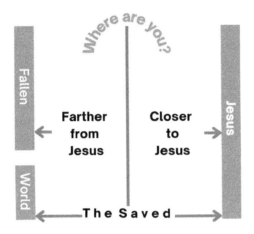

"What's your first impression of the drawing? Jack," Manny asked.

Jack thought before he spoke, a good habit for anyone who wants to live in God's Kingdom. "My eyes keep going to "Where are you?" He thought some more before he spoke. "It looks like I can be closer to Jesus or return to the fallen world I left behind. It was all me and the fallen world before I was saved on the way to catch my flight back to the States. Now it looks like I'm back in the Fallen World."

"You're missing something, Jack," Manny pointed out. "What does the title of the bottom line between Jesus and the Fallen World say?"

Jack looked. "It says 'The Saved.' I'm not understanding it. If I'm saved, I'm in the arms of Jesus, right? If I'm not saved, I'm in the place of the Fallen World. How can I be saved and far from Jesus at the same time?"

Jack had the same mistaken belief that many Christians have. "If I'm saved, have faith, and trust in Jesus, then He'll keep me safe from the world and myself. I admit I'm way too busy to seek Him with all my heart, but who isn't? Life is demanding. And, sure, I depend more on myself and the world than Him; after all, God helps those who help themselves, right? I can't be right next to Jesus all the time." Metaphorically speaking, that's like a starving person sitting before a banquet and not picking up his fork.

Manny got right to the point, like any good teacher does. "You only have to look at what's happened to you in the past six months to see the answer to your question. For the first year and a half of your new life, you were doing all the right things to stay near Jesus. You were very close to Him when you were feeding your spiritual self with the Word of God and prayer and Bible studies and all the other spiritual nourishment you were taking in. You were being His servant with your family, friends, and at work. Then you took your eyes off the prize and started going your own way—first by not spending the first hour of your day in prayer and worship and Scripture reading. Your job became more important to you than your relationship with God. Your family fell by the wayside as your life became all about you and the world. And Satan was having a field day with you because you were not depending on God your Father, Jesus your Savior, and the Holy Spirit your counselor. You were without spiritual armor to protect you. Shall I go on?"

Jack felt like a rumpled and tattered suit, once stitched together with top quality natural linen, a high thread count, and buttons made of horn.

"You don't need to go on. I know you know how far I've fallen; you seem to know everything about me. Please help me get out of this tailspin. I don't know what to do. I'm about ready to just give up. Do I need to be saved again?"

"That's a good place to be, Jack—at the point of giving up."

That further befuddled Jack. "How can that be a good place to be?"

"Because now you're ready to depend on someone other than yourself. What I'm *not* going to do, Jack, is be like a counselor and tell you to do this and do that. You need some depth of knowledge and understanding first."

Jack was wired up for whatever Manny had to say, as if his interior radio was tuned to *The Manny Station.*

"I'm ready," Jack said, and settled down into his seat with the electronic tablet in his lap.

"We're going to use that drawing you're looking at as a reference point, Jack. Listen carefully and ask questions if you need to."

Jack knew he was in God's classroom now. He reached into his own briefcase and brought out a leather binder with a legal pad in it. "If I'm a student in a classroom," he thought, "I'd better take lots of notes."

Jack had pen in hand, put in the date on the top left of the first page of the legal pad, and wrote, *Lesson from Manny on the Way to Chicago* under the date.

Manny started the lesson. "First of all, you don't need to be saved again. Once is enough. You're not back to the Fallen World, but you're living your life as if you were. You still have the Holy Spirit within you, and also Jesus and the Father. That's a good thing. But you have drifted so far away from God, that you have no idea where He is. Let's go back to the drawing and let me state the obvious. Not all positions within The Saved area of this drawing are equally safe, but then you've already found that out. The closer you are to Jesus, the safer you are. The closer to the Fallen World, the less safe you are and the more vulnerable to danger—like starting to drink again.

"In Paradise, Adam and Eve had a pure relationship with God and everything was very good. That's why it was the safest place on earth. But then came the fall and the curse and Paradise Lost—and death, disease, and destruction became inhabitants of the natural world permanently, even for those who are saved by the death and resurrection of Jesus Christ.

"After anyone is born-again from being children of Adam and Eve into being children of God, with Jesus Christ as their Savior, they are spiritually safe but not physically safe. There is still death for all, diseases that can ravage the body, and destruction in the way of storms, accidents, and wars. In short, Paradise Regained is not quite the same as Paradise Lost. One day it will be so, but not in this world. That's why it's really the second safest place on earth in the history of mankind. The operative message for the life of a Christian today was given to us by Jesus Himself in the last verse of the 16th chapter of John.

> In this world you will have trouble. But take
> heart! I have overcome the world.

"The trouble we have comes about because we live in a fallen world that is cursed. We're saved from the eternal consequences of the fall and are saved into a restored connection and relationship with God, but we're not saved from the consequences of the evil in this world. That's what Jesus meant in the verse I just quoted. There are wars, famines, floods, and terrible diseases like cancer. There are bad people who do great harm to good people. There are children who run away and spouses who get divorced. Businesses fail and jobs are lost. People become addicted to alcohol and drugs and their lives spiral out of control. That's what's happened to you, Jack. Should I go on?"

Jack was stunned by Manny's litany of the trouble in this world. "You're going right back to how I felt when we first met —all the danger and feeling hopeless. Where's the safety?"

"That may be the most intelligent question you've ever asked me." Manny paused. "And there are two very good answer I don't want you to ever forget.

"The safest place on earth is leaning back against Jesus, as John did in John 13:25. He referred to himself as the disciple Jesus loved. He doesn't say why, but perhaps he, more than the rest, understood the essentials of who Jesus really was and why He came and how His followers should respond to Him. I always recommend new Christians read John's gospel first because he answers those three essentials of *who*, *why*, and *how*.

Manny paused to let Jack finish his notes on the first answer before launching into the second.

"Again, the safest place in a dangerous world is being in a storm-swept boat about to sink, with Jesus who can calm the storm, as He did in Mark 4, verses 35-41. I want you to read that story every day for a month, until it becomes indelible in the traces of your mind.

"Look at the drawing again. The closer you are to Jesus, the safer you are, no matter how bad things are in your life. And the farther you are from Jesus, the more unsafe you are, no matter how good things are in your life. I also want you to look at that chart every day for a month. I'll send it as an attachment to your email.

Jack's pen was racing across the lines of his writing pad, depositing traces of ink where there had only been yellow paper.

"Though in this world, you can't be safe from a car accident or cancer, Jesus will help you cope with your troubles. However, you can be safer from your own addictions and inclinations and weaknesses. Even though you have a history of alcoholism, you can find safety in Jesus if you move away from yourself and the world and the temptations of Satan and toward Him. A man who is prone to anger and violence can find safety if he stays close to Jesus in the landscape shown in the drawing. But he's most unsafe and liable to make bad choices the more he drifts away from Jesus and toward the land of the Fallen World.

"Let's look to Proverbs 29:25 for another statement on the safest place on earth." Manny recited from the New King James version, which he preferred for this verse.

Whoever trusts in the LORD shall be safe.

"Safety is as close to Jesus in the chart you're looking at, Jack, as you can possibly get, bumping up against the vertical bar on the right. Billy Graham, one of the great evangelists of the last century, was exceedingly close to Jesus and was very safe as a result, though he died in the end. The Apostle Paul was as safe as safe could be, though he was beheaded in Rome, the same fate that the equally safe John the Baptist came to. A woman I know was in a comfortably safe place, though she died of cancer.

"A young man I know is also quite safe, though he is serving a prison term of 28 years for killing a woman when he was so high on meth that he didn't know what he was doing. He came to a county jail and tried to take his life any number of times—before he picked out a pocket Bible off a book cart, was led by the Holy Spirit to start reading in the Gospel of John, and became born-again in his cell. He went from sinner to saint in an instant, like the criminal on the cross next to Jesus.

"Now we come to the heart of the matter. The Spirit of Christ is fully present in the spirit of a believer, but his or her soul decides by its will how much possession it will allow Christ to have, and that's the basis for the chart you're looking at in the tablet.

"The Apostle John allowed Jesus a great deal of possession, as he and the world drifted to the edges of his soul. The Apostle Paul joyfully endured appalling hardships, fierce opposition, brutal beatings, threats on his life, and a thorn in his flesh because Christ's life was more important than his.

"Throughout history, from the time of Noah, we find men and women whose goal in life has been to stay near Jesus. We also find those professing to be Christians who are so far away from Jesus that they don't even know where He is or what He stands for. They are only concerned about themselves and their place in the world. As to the unsaved, they aren't part of the discussion.

"The woman dying of cancer was joyful to the end. The man serving 28 years in prison is one of the most joyful people I know. He calls me at least once a month to share his joy in the Lord. Never a complaint comes from his lips. A fellow inmate asked him, 'How can you be so happy when you will be in prison for most of the rest of your life?' He answered, 'Because I know Who is in here with me.'"

Jack looked up from his notepad and saw Manny closely watching him. "I think I'm starting to understand a bit. God hasn't moved; I've drifted. As to 'Where am I?' I'm dangerously close to where I was in the Fallen World. There can be no doubt. And that's why what happened to me has happened. I'm a Christian who's more interested in the world, myself, and having my own way instead of being led by Christ. It's been my way instead of God's way."

Jack didn't have the wherewithal to say what he just said—not the knowledge or the spiritual insight. It was beyond anything he could realize on his own. It was like a person quoting from a book he'd never read.

Manny knew what had just transpired; Jack didn't. The Holy Spirit had informed Jack to speak what he spoke. It was He who put the thoughts into his mind and the words on his lips.

Manny's whole face, from the top of his forehead to the bottom of his chin, became one big smile.

"At last you have it; you have stated it exceptionally well. It's as you've said. You're on the wrong side of the chart. The closer you've gotten to the bar on the left, the more you've become like the unsaved person you were.

"Get your pen ready to write down what I'm going to tell you now and then underline it, put a box around it, and imprint an asterisk on each side of it.

"This is not a once-and-for-all positioning. A person may be close to God in the morning during her devotional time and close to the Fallen World on her commute to work when someone cuts her off on the freeway and she swears at him. Or someone may be very near to Jesus during a Saturday morning Bible study and careening toward the other side of the chart when he comes home and has to pick up his teen-age daughter at the jail because she got caught with an ounce of a controlled substance.

"Do you get the picture, Jack? Where you are is not a one-time thing. A near-to-Jesus time can vanish in an instant. You must have a firm foundation in Christ and be ever vigilant throughout the day to stay near God. It needs to be Jesus in the morning, Jesus at noontime, Jesus in the afternoon, and Jesus at night."

Jack wrote furiously, underlined dramatically, put a bold box around what he had written, and marked giant asterisks on the top and bottom and on both sides. When he finished, he looked over at Manny, who had been waiting patiently.

"I get the picture," he said simply. "But what do I do about it? How do I stay next to God 24 hours a day?"

The voice of the plane's captain came over the speaker system. "This is your captain speaking. Prepare for landing."

Manny reached over for his tablet that Jack had and put it in his briefcase, along with his Bible. "That will be the subject of our next meeting."

Jack had learned not to ask when that would be. It would happen when it happened. Fifteen minutes later they deplaned. Jack headed toward the baggage claim. Manny went in the opposite direction.

Lesson Six

After a 10 a.m. meeting with the president and board of the medical center, Jack strolled over to the Bond Chapel on the University of Chicago campus, some two blocks away. Marianne had told him he simply had to see it if he had a chance. She had graduated from the University of Chicago, and the chapel was like a second home to her.

The outside of the chapel presented an impressive Gothic Revival architecture, and the interior had a massive pipe organ and magnificent stained glass windows. The movable blue chairs were set in a perpendicular-to-the-front-of-the-chapel arrangement, with three rows on one side of a six-brick walkway facing three rows on the other side. Jack sat in a chair near the front and thought about the lesson learned from Manny the previous day on the airplane.

For whatever reason, which was unusual for a noontime, no one else was in the chapel. Jack was glad for the quiet and slipped into a meditative state for ten minutes before he heard the clicking of familiar footsteps on the brick walkway coming closer and closer.

Manny was dressed in a blue suit with an expensive white shirt and red tie. He sat down on the first chair opposite Jack. "Thinking about yesterday's graph?" Manny asked, capturing exactly what Jack was thinking about. "Would you like to find out how to stay near God 24 hours a day, as you asked yesterday?"

"I would," Jack answered, "but I suppose I'd need to cut out eight hours for sleep."

"Maybe so," Manny said, "and maybe not." That answer surprised Jack, but he wasn't about to ask about it. There was a more important lesson coming.

Manny pulled his Bible out of the briefcase he always had with him. He left the tablet where it was.

"What do you see in my hand?" Manny asked Jack.

"A Bible," Jack answered.

Manny straightened and tightened his red tie, and the lesson began.

"Okay, Jack, if you want to stay near God, you want to know all about Him. And where might you find that?"

Jack didn't want to take the chance he might be wrong, so his answer came out more like a question.

"In the Bible you're holding?"

"Exactly. Would you please turn to 2 Timothy 3:16 in your Bible and read it out loud." Jack did so.

> All Scripture is God-breathed and is useful
> for teaching, rebuking, correcting, and training in
> righteousness.

"How do you see that verse applying to you?" Manny asked.

Jack answered the question with a question. "Can I ask a few questions first?"

"Of course. Always."

"What does God-breathed mean?"

"That's an excellent question, Jack. Let me give you some background information. The Bible was written over a period of roughly two-thousand years by forty different authors from three continents who wrote in three different languages. Shepherds, kings, scholars, fishermen, prophets, a military general, a cupbearer, and a priest all penned portions of Scripture. Yet, despite this mixed bag of writers and settings, the Bible displays a meticulous consistency. It never contradicts itself or its common theme.

"That could only happen if the real author of the Bible were not forty natural men but God Himself, working through His Holy Spirit to inspire each and every one of those forty. The common thread running throughout the Bible is Jesus Christ and Him crucified. The Old Testament prophets were writing about Someone in the future without knowing in their natural selves who exactly they were writing about."

Jack pondered this, and Manny patiently waited for a response.

"So, essentially, God wrote the Bible and if we want to know Him personally, we need to read His Word ..." Jack closed his eyes for three seconds and opened them again to finish his last sentence. "... a lot. But that brings up another dilemma. If I read the Bible a lot, I need to know how to go about it. I expect that's the lesson you're going to teach me right now. Let's start with how often I should be reading the Bible—every day, all of the time, or what?"

Manny was ready for that question and pulled an Amplified Old Testament out of his briefcase, opened it up to Joshua 1:8, and read. He wanted to use the Amplified version because of its expanded translation of the original Hebrew:

> This Book of the Law shall not depart from
> your mouth, but you shall read [and meditate on]
> it day and night, so that you may be careful to do
> [everything] in accordance with all that is written in
> it; for then you will make your way prosperous, and
> then you will be successful.

"Does that answer your question? All the time isn't specific enough. Day and night gives a better guideline."

"Another question," said Jack. "Does meditate mean to think over what I'm reading? Up to six months ago, I was reading the Bible daily, but I wasn't meditating or studying or being careful to do everything in it. Then I stopped reading it altogether."

"I know that, Jack. I also know that even before you stopped reading it altogether, you were skimming through the Bible as if you were reading a novel. In the end, you were reading the Bible as if it were a ritual to perform, without enthusiasm or seeking to learn anything about God."

Jack shook his head in dismay. "But the Bible's so boring. I started with Genesis and was geared up to read through Revelation. Genesis and Exodus were exciting, but the next three books were monotonous and uninteresting. All that stuff about sacrifices and building a tabernacle and wandering around in a desert for forty years was like reading a chemistry book. When I got into Samuel, Kings, and Chronicles, it was all about the history of people I'd never heard about, except for David and Solomon.

Manny countered. "That's what I've been telling you, Jack. You were reading the Bible like a novel. You started in the beginning and were going to read through to the end. But that's not a very good plan."

Jack countered. "Then what is a good plan?"

"I'd suggest you start with the Gospel of John in the New Testament and Genesis in the Old, reading back and forth between the two of them. Then read through Matthew, Mark, and Luke; and Exodus, the Psalms, and Isaiah in the Old Testament, in the same back and forth manner. We can discuss where to go after that. If you search online for *Read through the Bible in a year*, you'll find all sorts of plans.

Manny continued. "You should have two different times to study Scripture—one for the New Testament and one for the Old."

Jack wasn't ready for that much Bible reading. The morning was enough for him. He challenged Manny, and not in a very nice way.

"What? How am I going to find time to do that? You know I've got a job and a family. Right now it's easy to read the Bible when I'm traveling—on the plane, in my hotel room, between appointments, and stuff like that. But I'm home more than half the time."

"There'll never be the time to read Scripture if you try to shoehorn it into your daily life. You need to take time from something else."

"Like what?"

"What time does your family get up in the morning?"

"About 7 O'clock."

"Then you can get up at 6:00 and spend an hour in prayer and studying John and the other three gospels."

"I was getting up at 6:00 until a month ago, but, like I told you, it became so boring that I had to drag myself out of bed."

"Do you even know why you're reading the Bible, Jack?"

It was a sharp question and not one Jack had anticipated. It took him aback and his answer was quite stupid.

"Because you told me to."

"That's a dismal reason for reading the Bible, Jack. It's a wonder you made it as far as you did."

Jack had a look on his face that showed he didn't have any idea why he should read the Bible, so Manny's job was to enlighten him.

"The Bible is the filter for how we see God, how we see others, and how we see ourselves. You say you want to follow Jesus, but to do so can't be based solely on your observations or what you hear in church on a Sunday or anything else in your experience. You need to see Jesus with spiritual eyes. You need to see God as He wants you to see Him. That's the purpose of reading the Bible.

"Your view of God without reading His Word is like being married to a woman you've never seen. Jesus came not just to change our eternal destination but to make a difference in how we see the world we live in and our very selves. In fact, that's what the whole Bible is about, starting with Genesis.

"You've been reading the Bible from your own perspective. That's why it's boring to you. If you read it from God's perspective, the Bible is the most exciting book that's ever been written. Scripture will help you see your addiction differently and will help change your perspective on the meaning of life, from the inside-out. The *I AM* will turn your life upside down and make you into the man God wants you to be."

Manny echoed what Jack had just said. "Yes, for the most part, you were just going through the motions, following a schedule because that's what I told you to do, skimming the surface of Scripture but avoiding the depth. Let me ask you, 'What do you do after supper?'"

"I watch TV until I go to bed. It relaxes me."

"Take a half hour at the end of your TV watching and before you go to bed at night and study Genesis, Exodus, Psalms, and Isaiah."

"I'd been going to bed right after watching a couple of shows so I could get up early the next morning for worship time." Jack paused. "But then I stopped getting up early the next morning and slept in to 7 a.m. So I could have done the half hour then, but if I go back to getting up at 6:00, how will I have time to read the Bible at night and still get enough sleep? I need my sleep or I'm no good the next day."

"Tape the shows on the night they air and watch them the next night. You'll save 15 minutes just by skipping the commercials. Taping two programs will give you the half hour you need."

"I never thought of that," Jack said. "I guess I could do that."

It's interesting that Jack had his hand on his Bible when he agreed to Manny's suggestion.

Manny continued. "No matter what else you do, just reading the Bible according to a plan is one of the most important things you can do, if not the most important.

"But ..." Manny hesitated, even though he knew exactly what he was going to say next, "you don't want to read the Bible like a magazine or newspaper. God speaks to us through His Word, and you want to listen closely. And that's not the end of it. You also want to discover the meaning of what you're reading as it applies to your own life and contemplate how to put it into practice."

Jack sat with his lips parted but no words came out at first. Finally he spoke.

"That's too much coming at me all at once. I feel buried."

"I can understand that, Jack. Let me give you an example from everyday life to see if that helps sort it out."

"Okay. I'm curious as to what it will be."

"Do you remember when you got your driver's license in high school?"

"Absolutely. Then I could go places without having to hound my parents for a ride."

"Did someone just hand you the driver's license one day?"

"Of course not. I learned the rules of the road in a manual I picked up at the license place downtown."

"Did you just read through it once?"

"More like ten times. I studied hard until I knew everything in it because I had to take a written test, which I aced."

"And then they gave you your driver's license?"

"Not quite. I had to pass a driving test too, you know, driving a car with a license officer checking me out."

"Did you take that test as soon as you passed the written test?"

"Well, no. I had to practice on the road with a driving instructor until she told me I was ready for the test. And when I passed it, I received my driver's license."

Those were exactly the answers Manny had expected to hear, and his response had been determined before they met in the chapel.

"That's the way it is with reading the Bible, Jack. It's your driver's manual. You don't want to just read through the Bible. You want to study it as if you're going to take an exam.

"Then you want to practice applying it to your life like you practiced driving a car on the road. Then, and only then, can you be confident that you know where you're going in the Kingdom of God and how to get there. In effect, the Bible is your road map. Does it make sense now?"

"It seems to make sense now, but how do I do that? Do I just read through it over and over like a driver's manual?" Jack sighed. "Wow, I must really seem stupid."

"You're not stupid, Jack. You're uninformed. My job is to inform you. I'd suggest you buy a Study Bible to help with the studying part of it."

"My wife has one of those, but it's for women."

"You can find a good Study Bible for everyone or just for men or just for addicts in a Christian bookstore or online, like Amazon."

"I suppose I can do that."

His hand remained on his Bible.

"What else? You said I shouldn't be reading Scripture like reading a magazine. How *should* I read it?"

"Good question. You should be thinking about what you're reading and praying on it."

"Praying on it? What's that mean?"

"You know, Jack, I think it might be better to show you what I mean instead of telling you, okay?"

"I think it would be too."

Would be better? Try telling a child how to ride a bike without showing them. Or how to swim without being with them in the water. Would be turns into must be.

"Turn to the Gospel of John and read the first two verses of the first chapter." Jack turned to the verses and read.

> In the beginning was the Word, and the Word
> was with God, and the Word was God. He was with
> God in the beginning.

"The Word is Jesus Christ in this passage, and Jesus was both with God and always was God right from the beginning. So when you pray to Jesus, you're automatically praying to God. In John 10:30, Jesus says, I and the Father are one. This is the mystery of the trinity that can't be adequately explained in our three-dimensional world."

Manny paused for effect. Jack was motionless, as if he were in a spell of some kind.

"Here's one way you could think about and pray about these two verses.

> "Lord Jesus, thank You for being the Word
> and for coming down on earth to die for our sins.
> You are a great God. You are a mighty God. I know
> I can't understand You completely, but it gives me
> great hope just to know that You're God. I love You
> Jesus for who You are and what You did for me, my
> God and my Savior."

The look on Jack's face told Manny he'd gotten through.

"Wow!" I never would have thought about doing something like that."

"Do you want to give it a try, Jack, let's say with John 14:1?"

That's the very verse Jack would have chosen given enough time. He had visited it often because it spoke to his ongoing anxiety. He recited it from memory.

> "Do not let your hearts be troubled. Trust in
> God; trust also in Me."

"I'll give it the good old college try, but don't expect anything great out of me."

He took in three deep breaths, and the Holy Spirit took
that time to guide him.

> "Father God, my heart is troubled because of
> my seeing danger everywhere and my failings with
> my family and my drinking and my drifting away
> from you. I've messed up royally and can't pull my-
> self out of the spiral I'm in. This verse tells me I can
> turn it all over to you, and that's what I'm going to
> do. I thank you for putting Manny in my life. I don't
> know what I'd do without him. How can I not trust
> You and trust Jesus? I don't pray this on my own,
> Father God, but in Jesus' name."

It was one of those awesome times in life when words are
spoken from an otherworldly place in a person's being. Jack
prayed as if he'd been handed a script by the Holy Spirit, which
in a way he had. Manny sat silent and motionless for the time
it would take to say, "Praise God from whom all blessings flow."

"Jack, I don't know what to say," which was a first for
Manny. "That was a marvelous prayer that you put in your
own language. I'm impressed, and I believe God is very pleased
with it as well."

Manny chose not to tell Jack that the Holy Spirit was
praying through him at that moment because it would have
been a distraction from the main lesson.

"It's time to wrap up this lesson. You've enough information to get you going with reading the Bible. And, as you
commit yourself to a plan to be nourished by God's Word, He'll
reveal to you insights and revelations beyond anything I can
teach you.

"Let's meet again in about three weeks to see how you're
doing with your Bible-reading plan. And I'll give you a lesson

on the next strategy to stay close to God. What do you think that will be, Jack?"

"I'm not sure," Jack answered, but, in fact, he was more sure than he let on.

"Then think about it and pray on it, and we'll see what you come up with."

Jack opened his smartphone to check his calendar. "I'll be in Ireland in three weeks, he said."

"Yes, I know," Manny replied.

Both of them got up and walked to the front door of the Bond Chapel. Outside, on the sidewalk, Jack went to the right and Manny to the left.

Manny walked on the sidewalk. Jack walked on a cloud. He was inspired and fired up to read the Bible in a way he never had before. Everything Manny had said excited him. He made a commitment in his heart to exactly follow Manny's direction for reading Scripture. His life would never be the same, he felt. That night he called Marianne, filled to the brim with joy, to tell her he had a new way to read the Bible and explained it to her. She had been reading the Bible like that for years but hadn't shared that with her husband. She rejoiced with him.

Lesson Seven

Three weeks to the day, Jack was back in Dublin to meet with the medical administration of St. James Hospital in the afternoon at 2 p.m. The next day he'd be heading down to Cork to meet with a similar group from the Bon Secours Health System. His day started at 9 a.m. Matins in St. Patrick's Cathedral. On his way back to his hotel near Christ Church Cathedral, there was a little café, and Jack stopped in for a latte and a piece of soda bread. He watched the passersby pass by the window table where he sat, which was away from the hustle and bustle of the rest of the shop.

First by was a small group of uniformed girls, heading south to their classes at a private school across from St. Patrick's. Then a steady parade of tourists, who had also been at Matins, heading north to who knows where in their quest to see everything they could of what Dublin had to offer. Jack stopped people watching to write a thought in his notebook regarding Psalm 73, which had been read at the recent service. When he looked up again, there was Manny standing in front of the window looking down at him, with his leather briefcase at his side and a look of mirth that put his eyes into a squint as his cheeks rose to meet them.

"May I come in?" Manny mouthed.

Jack extended his right arm out and drew it back twice with his palm up, a universal sign for "Come on in."

Shortly after Manny sat down at Jack's table, a waitress brought him exactly what Jack had ordered.

There was rarely any small talk with Manny. No "How are you doing?" or "What's been happening in your life?" He got right down to business, in this case a discussion of how Jack's Bible reading was progressing. It had gone quite well for the first two weeks. Then the shine came off, and Jack labored to maintain his enthusiasm and dedication. As often happens with such commitments, the demands and distractions of life got in the way, like thorns growing up and choking a plant. Jack didn't notice any of that, however, because the slipping away had been a gradual slope.

"My Bible reading's been going well," Jack said, in a way a person might say he was sticking with an exercise plan that had been a good idea at the time but was now getting burdensome. He smiled. Just meeting with Manny buoyed his spirit, and he told his heart he'd renew his enthusiasm for studying the Bible and meditating on it, not just going through the motions. Manny was like a new spark igniting a smoldering fire. He brought out the best in Jack's soul.

Manny knew that Jack's dedication reflected duty more than devotion. He had seen that pattern many times before. At this time, however, he chose to be encouraging rather than critical, though with less than wholehearted praise. "I applaud you for sticking with reading the Bible twice a day, Jack. Just keep in mind that you're not reading the morning or evening newspaper. You're studying the living Word of God."

Jack's spirit and soul were perforated by Manny's reminder. "I'll do better," Jack thought. "I know I can do better, and I will." Manny had that effect on him.

"Now we start our next lesson, and you already know what that will be, don't you?"

Jack didn't wonder any more how Manny would know that. He simply knew that he knew, but how that happened, he didn't know.

Manny opened his Bible to Luke 5:16 and read.

> But Jesus often withdrew to lonely places and
> prayed.

"What do you think Jesus prayed about?" Manny asked.

"I don't know," Jack answered. "How would I?" It came out as a smart-alecky remark, and Jack immediately regretted saying it.

Manny took no note of the sarcasm and sipped his latte

as if it were ten degrees beyond hot. "You wouldn't, and the Bible doesn't say. But the more you learn about Jesus, the better you can imagine what he might have been praying about. First of all, it's safe to conclude that Jesus' prayers didn't follow the pattern of how the world prays."

Jack took a bite of his bread. "And how does the world pray?" This time his words were respectful and sincere.

"I'm glad you asked that," Manny answered, as he pulled a Lifeway Research survey out of his briefcase and started reading it. This survey reported that nearly half of Americans pray every day. As for what they're praying for:

- 82 percent pray for friends and family.
- 74 percent pray for their own needs and difficulties.
- 42 percent pray for their own sins.
- 38 percent pray for those stricken by natural disasters.
- About 20 percent pray to win the lottery, for no one to find out about a bad thing they did, for God to avenge someone who hurt them or a loved one, or for their favorite team to win a game.
- About 10 percent pray for bad things to happen to bad people, to not get caught speeding, or to find a parking spot."

Jack didn't hesitate with his response. "The first four don't sound too bad, but the last two are pretty lame."

"Do you think this is all there is to prayer, Jack? Do you think this is how Jesus taught His disciples to pray?"

Jack shook his head back and forth. "By the tone of your voice and the pointedness of your two questions, I'm going to have to give a firm no. But don't ask me what I think Jesus taught His disciples or what prayer is really about. You're the teacher, and I'm the student."

With that, Jack pulled out his notebook and pen and swiveled himself into a writing posture. The lesson on prayer was about to begin.

"First question," Manny declared, "is how often to pray. What do you think the answer to that is, Jack?"

Jack pondered the question with an empty look on his face, like no one was home in his mind. Then a light dawned and was reflected on his face.

"Last time we met, the answer to how often to read the Bible was daily, in fact, twice a day. I'm going to guess that setting aside two times a day to pray meets your quota."

Manny had the look of a teacher whose students came up with a less-than-adequate answer to a question.

"I don't have a quota for prayer," Manny said. "The Bible does." He opened up to 2 Corinthians 5:17 and recited the verse while looking at Jack and not the page before him.

Pray without ceasing.

Jack was taken by surprise and spoke without any interruption of thought. He had not slept well the night before, partly due to the six-hour difference in time and partly due to his mind contemplating the bottom-line meeting coming up. It didn't take much for him to abandon courtesy and civility, even with Manny.

"How is that even possible? You wouldn't be able to do anything except pray all day long. It's unrealistic."

Manny reacted gently to Jack's outburst. "Let's try another translation," he ventured, still not looking down at his Bible. "Several Bibles say, 'Pray continually.' I think that's more what the Apostle Paul had in mind."

Jack calmed down a couple notches but was still combative. "That's still a stretch," he said. "I can just see someone walking around all day mumbling to God and not getting anything else done. They'd go in the books as a crazy person."

Manny's patience came to an abrupt end. His voice raised up several decibels and snapped with a sharpness Jack hadn't heard before. "Stop it, Jack! You don't know what you're talking about. Are you so slow to learn about looking to God in all things and not being caught up in your own worldly thinking? Who are you to question Scripture? Who are you to say no one can pray continually? The Bible is truth. Jesus taught the Apostle Paul for three years in the desert. If he says to pray continually, your job is to figure out what that means, not question it." Several heads in the café turned to look when they heard Manny's outburst. However, they were too far away to catch exactly what he said.

Jack felt as he had when his father backhanded him at fifteen years old, after he told his mother he wished she'd drop dead and stop nagging him. He was humiliated then and deeply ashamed now, and his propriety returned to him.

"I'm sorry, Manny. There's still too much of Jack in Jack. Please forgive me. I'm going to put me on the back burner and listen to what you have to teach." The gloves were off, the fists unclenched, the arms hung limply down his side.

Manny was not one to hold grudges. "I forgive you, Jack, and I'm sorry I had to be so harsh with you, but you left me no choice. You need to get yourself turned around 180 degrees."

With a sad face and a slumped body, Jack nodded his head. He was now in submissive mode, exactly the place he needed to be.

"Let's look at what Paul meant by praying continually," Manny said. "He didn't mean Christians should walk around all day mumbling to God, as you put it. He didn't mean they should abandon carrying on with a normal life and do nothing but pray.

"What Paul meant was that you can live in a constant attitude of prayer, even as you go about your daily routines. Some days you'll pray much more than others, of course, but you can be in a continual attitude of prayer. Regardless of what's on your 'To Do' list, you can have an ongoing conversation with the Lord who desires to be involved in your whole life, from the inside out, including the little mundane circumstances of life, like taking out the garbage on Wednesday night." How did Manny know that Jack did indeed take out the garbage on Wednesday night?

"God is interested in every part of your life, from the time you brush your teeth in the morning to the time you pull the covers back at night. He wants to know your interests and your concerns. He invites you to talk to Him when you are confused or frightened or facing challenges in your life, both big and small. Your trying to find a lost magazine is not insignificant to Him.

"If you are concerned about your wife's visit to the doctor, He is even more concerned; she is one of His faithful daughters. Whomever or whatever you intercede for in prayer, He hears it like a knock on His door.

"As you seek His presence here and there and everywhere, you'll find Him. He is in the fireplace downstairs during your morning worship time. He is in your office upstairs when you start your workday. He is in the kitchen where you eat and in the bedroom where you sleep. He is everywhere outside and in every home, store, or building where you set your foot. Wherever you go, He is there first. You don't lose Him when you fly or ride in a taxi or wait for a business meeting.

"He's here in this shop with us while we meet. Do you feel His presence?"

Jack was now sitting bolt upright in his chair and taking in every word Manny spoke, as if he were receiving bars of gold to put in his suitcase for the trip home. "Yes, I feel God's presence. You've brought Him here with you."

"No, Jack," Manny said. "He was here with you before I came in. What I did was point Him out to you, to show you what you already had but were not aware of. You don't need me, Jack, to find Jesus. He lives in you through the power of the Holy Spirit. It's like the important business report you couldn't find in your office before you went to the airport yesterday. It was in your office with you, but you had forgotten where you put it. You searched for it like the widow searching for her lost coin, and when you found it you rejoiced. While it was still lost would have been a good time to pray and trust God that you'd find it, instead of being in a panic and snapping at your wife.

"My prayer for you, Jack, is that, through an ongoing communication with God, you will fall in love with Jesus and see Him as the King in your life and relish His goodness, faithfulness, and wonderful direction for you. And that you will find strength and wisdom for every turn in your path throughout every day, so you can experience all He has created you for.

When you develop this prayerful outlook, when indeed you become a man of prayer, your communication with the Lord will become your first instinct in every situation. I pray that in time, it will never occur to you not to pray. Now do you understand what it means to pray continually?"

Jack had a look of joy and a question mark on his face at the same time, if that's even possible.

"Yes, I guess I do now that you've explained it. I feel like a fool for questioning Scripture. I won't make that mistake again."

Jack caught his breath and deliberated on what to say next after completing his confession.

"I hope the next part of the lesson is about how to pray and what to pray about."

"But of course, Jack," Manny reassured him. "The lesson on prayer is only half over. We had to deal with the why and how first; now we'll take up the what and the when."

Jack had been at the front of his chair. Now he sat back with pen in hand and notebook on lap to memorialize the wisdom Manny was about to impart to him.

Manny turned around to look at the clock on the back wall. It was 10:45. "Jack, you have an important meeting at 2 p.m., and you need to prepare for it as if it were going to be the biggest single sale of your company this year. You'll be meeting in the administrative building; your meeting will finish at 4 p.m. sharp. After that, head over to the main entrance of St. James. When you come in the front door, you'll see a reception desk in front of you and a Londis store to the left. On the terrace above that store, I'll be sitting at a round table with two chairs. We'll have the area to ourselves.

"I want to quickly set the theme for that meeting with three verses from three of the gospels. The first is Luke 6:12, the second is Mark 1:35, and the last is Matthew 4:12." Manny flipped his Bible open and read the passages in less than a minute.

One of those days Jesus went out to a mountainside to pray, and spent the night praying to God.

Very early in the morning, while it was still dark, Jesus got up, left the house and went off to a solitary place, where he prayed.

Then Jesus was led by the Spirit into the wilderness ... [for] forty days and forty nights.

"The point I'm making, Jack, is that Jesus knew how to pray, and He's the best source for us to know how to pray. See you at 4:30."

With that, Manny left the café and Jack went back to his hotel to prepare.

Lesson Eight

The meeting at St. James concluded at exactly 4 p.m., and it did end up to be the largest sale for Jack's company that year, by a lot. Jack walked down to the lobby of the administrative building and settled down on a bench by the front window. His cell phone went bing-bing-bing with text messages from headquarters, where it was 10 a.m. in the morning. They had just seen the proposed sale posted, and if a text message could gasp, theirs were gasping. Congratulations was the operative word of the texts. Jack didn't tell them that Manny had called it.

Jack stepped through the main entrance of St. James at 4:27 p.m. and saw Manny sitting on the terrace above the Londis convenience shop, at a circular wire-top table with two chairs you'd expect to see in a fast-food restaurant. Three minutes later, Jack was sitting across from him. Manny smiled a greeting as Jack pulled his notebook and pen out. Manny didn't ask about Jack's recent rewarding meeting, and Jack said nothing about it.

"Well, Jack, are you ready for Part Two of the lesson on prayer?"

"I am," Jack replied. "I read the three Bible verses we ended with this morning, just before I walked over here. I have to admit I'm not very good at praying. I'm ready to ramp up my game."

Jack ended at that point. Manny looked at him for several seconds before saying, "And?"

"And I'm all ears to find out what Jesus has to say about prayer." Jack paused. "I expect that the Lord's Prayer fits in there someplace?"

Manny straightened his tie and smoothed his sport coat,

just like someone of distinction about to make a presentation to an auditorium of 4,000 people.

"It fits in there right at the top," Manny said. "We find the Lord's Prayer in the 5th chapter of Matthew. You've been saying that prayer since your mother taught it to you as a young boy."

"How did Manny know that?" Jack thought to himself, but he didn't ask him out loud.

Manny continued. "You'll notice I used the words, 'Saying that prayer,' because that's what you've been doing. You've not been praying it in the way Jesus meant it to be prayed." Jack didn't ask what Manny meant by that, any more than a member of the audience of 4,000 would jump up and ask the presenter a question. He waited patiently for the lesson to be opened up, like a piece of paper that had been folded six times.

"You see, Jack, the Lord's Prayer is meant to be a prayer outline or framework more so than a prayer in itself. Like the outline of a book is not the book itself, or the framework of a house is not the house itself.

"What if I told you that you could pray the Lord's Prayer once through for at least an hour? And what if I told you that you could pray it again later in the day with different thoughts and words? And what if I told you that you could pray one part of it to start the day and another part driving to work and another part during a quiet time in your office?"

This time Jack responded, though he knew it was a rhetorical question. He couldn't help himself. "I'd say you know something I don't."

"Well, Jack, why don't I tell you what I know that you don't."

Manny already had his electronic notebook on the table, opened it to the fifth graphic, and turned it toward Jack.

"This is a house of prayer, Jack, and these seven boards, nailed to vertical studs behind them, make up the framework. In spiritual terms, they are called petitions."

The drawing was not a graphic masterpiece. Manny had drawn it roughly and quickly to serve as a reference for Jack. He didn't intend for it to hang in an art gallery.

Our Father Who
are in Heaven

Hallowed be
Thy Name

Thy Kingdom
come

Thy Will be done on earth
as it is in Heaven

Give us this day
our daily bread

And forgive our sins as we forgive
those who sin against us

And lead us not into temptation
but deliver us from evil.

"Each of these seven boards represents one petition of the Lord's prayer. The top one is called *Our Father Who are in Heaven*. This is our cue to declare that God is far above us, and His ways are greater than our ways, and His thoughts greater than our thoughts. We can also declare that Jesus is our King, who is also in heaven and within us through the power of the Holy Spirit, and that at His name every knee will bow and every tongue will acknowledge God. This is also a good place to promise that we'll go God's way instead of our own way."

Jack's eyes lit up like night lights. "I see. I get it, I think. You use the words of the Lord's prayer as hints of what to pray about. It doesn't have to be praying about yourself or others all the time." He started writing furiously in his notebook.

"You're absolutely right, Jack. The first four petitions of the Lord's prayer are about Him and the last three are about you."

The Holy Spirit joined the conversation as Manny and Jack discussed another ten ways to pray about our Father in Heaven, ending with thanking Him for being our God and for creating us in His image and likeness.

It was time for the next board—*Hallowed be Thy name*.

"What do you think the second one means, Jack?"

Jack understood the process and didn't hesitate.

"I imagine it means this is where we praise God and worship Him, right, like at the beginning of a church service? And we'd praise and worship Jesus too, right?"

"Right again. It would be helpful for you to know some of the names of God so you can pray more specifically. Manny reached into his briefcase and pulled out a sheet of paper that he had printed off a Navigator's website. Here are 30 names for you. You could pray a new one every day."

1.	Jehovah
2.	Jehovah-M'Kaddesh
3.	Infinite
4.	Omnipotent
5.	Good
6.	Love
7.	Jehovah-Jireh
8.	Jehovah-Shalom
9.	Immutable
10.	Transcendent
11.	Just
12.	Holy
13.	Jehovah-Raphe
14.	Self-Sufficient
15.	Omniscient
16.	Omnipresent
17.	Merciful
18.	Sovereign
19.	Jehovah-Nissi
20.	Wise
21.	Faithful
22.	Wrathful
23.	Full of Grace
24.	Our Comforter
25.	El-Shaddai
26.	Father
27.	The Church's Head
28.	Our Intercessor
29.	Adonai
30.	Elohim

"Are you going to tell me what the Hebrew names mean?" Jack asked.

Manny gave him a mischievous smile. "Look them up," he said.

"How about *Thy kingdom come*? "Manny asked. What ideas do you have on that?"

Jack thought before answering.

"Does that mean when Jesus comes again at the end of time, like the Bible says?"

"That's part of it, Jack. What else?"

Jack's vacant look indicated the state of his mind.

Manny offered him a lifeline. "The Kingdom of God has come to you, right?"

"Right."

"You can thank God for dying on the cross so His kingdom could come to you."

"Got it," Jack said.

"Do you have friends or family members who aren't saved?"

"Too many of them," Jack answered.

"Then you can pray for The Kingdom of God to come to them and ask what you can do to help that happen."

Jack's mind began to fill with understanding. "That's probably better than asking God to heal their sicknesses and take care of their problems, right?"

"Exactly. What good is health in this life if eternal damnation is waiting on the other side of the curtain?"

"Got it," Jack said. "Should we move on to the next petition?"

"We have a bit more work to do on this one, Jack. There's one more thing to add to your notes."

"Okay, I'm ready," Jack said, as his pen hovered over the notepad on the table in front of him.

"Here it is. Christ-followers don't march on their own to their own cadence. They're attached to the Army of the Lord to help advance the Kingdom of God on earth while their hearts still beat.

"This is where you ask God how you can advance His kingdom this day. Who can you talk to? Who can you disciple? Who can you serve? If it weren't for this part of the Lord's Prayer, I wouldn't be talking to you today in this hospital."

Manny didn't say anything more until Jack caught up with his note taking.

"I've got it all down," Jack said. "Now do we move to *Thy*

will be done?" Jack, as was his natural inclination, stepped out of the teacher-student role and advanced his own impulsive thinking. "This is where we pray to follow God's will, right? As in I ask that God's will be done in me. His will isn't for me to go back to emptying whiskey bottles, so when I pray for His will to be done, I'm really praying for Him to take away my craving to drink and keep me away from Satan's temptations."

Manny put up his hand to stop Jack from rattling on senselessly. "Jack, you're treating God like a vending machine. Do this for me; do that for me. Stop my drinking. Help my family. Love me more. You're treating Jesus like a little puppy dog, asking Him to follow you around and do your bidding. That's not the way prayer works. That's not the way this petition works."

If you can picture what a balloon filled with air looks like after someone pokes a pin into it, you'd have a good idea of what Jack looked like after Manny's admonishment. Jack sat silent; he had nothing more to say.

"Jack, listen carefully. Praying for God's will to be done doesn't mean asking Him to follow you around and take care of your problems. It means you seek out His will and follow Him around to be His hands extended. You've been asking God, 'Come into my world and help me live in it, and I'll be a shining light for You.' You need to turn 180 degrees and listen to Him say, 'No, you come into My Kingdom and I'll show you how to live in it and I'll be a shining light for you.'"

Jack sat like a sponge soaking up what Manny told him. He absorbed every word. He took no notes at this point.

Manny went on. "There are things we know are in God's will and things we don't. Reading the Bible every day and praying continually are a couple examples of knowing God's will. Also, praying for the salvation of a family member or friend are in God's will. What you don't know is whether your brother getting what seems like the perfect job is in God's will for him or not. You don't know if praying for your best friend's wife to be cured of cancer will be what's best for her. It may be that she'll come to Christ because of her disease, and you'd be praying for her to not be saved. Do you see what I mean, Jack?"

Jack nodded his head, like a serf before a king, and remained silent.

"For example, you can pray God's will be done with your family, friends, co-workers, and people you meet every day. You can pray for peace and encouragement for them and for godly people to minister to them, including yourself.

"You don't have to offer God a strategy for your brother. You can simply pray something like this, 'Lord, my brother needs a new job, but he needs something more important. He needs your saving grace to be born again. If this is the job where that might somehow happen, I pray You show him favor. If another job would be better for that, I pray for that job to roll in.'

"And for your nephew who's hoping that the coach of his high school football team will choose him to be the starting quarterback, 'Lord, protect the health of my nephew wherever he ends up. Build a hedge of protection around him both in his physical pursuits and in his spiritual development. If being quarterback would be the best thing for him, I pray You help pave the way. If another position might fit the talents You gave him better, help him see what your will is for him.' Does this make sense to you, Jack?"

Jack suddenly found his voice. "That's a whole new way of praying. I shouldn't be praying for my will to be done. I mean, like how do I know what's best for my brother or my nephew. God knows what's best, and that's what I should be praying for."

Now it was Manny's turn to remain silent. He showed what it meant to grin from ear to ear. It was time to move on to the next board.

Manny straightened his tie for the fourth time. "The first four boards have to do with God; the last three with us. "What're your thoughts on *Give us this day our daily bread*?"

"Well, given what stupid answers I've been giving, I think I'll just listen to what you have to say instead."

Manny gave an encouraging smile. "Good choice. You could have said it means God providing you with food, shelter, clothing, and all the other things you need to live that day. And you'd be right. "

Jack nodded. That's exactly what he'd have said.

"What's the name of the devotional your wife, Marianne, reads every morning?"

Jack thought for a moment. "I don't remember."

"I do," Manny replied. "It's called Our Daily Bread."

"That's it," Jack said.

"Our daily bread means your spiritual food for the day, which is actually more important than your physical needs. Bible reading and prayer are your spiritual food but so too is your asking God to put people in your life who will provide spiritual nourishment for you. And situations and circumstances that will help you grow in Christ.

"And this is where you can pray for spiritual nourishment for others in your sphere of influence. For example, this is the place in the Lord's Prayer where you pray for Aunt Mable's arthritis, your cousin Jack's drug addiction, and your sister Mary's breakup with her husband."

Jack was armed with new information as he ventured, "You mean in the way we pray about God's will, right? I used to pray that God would heal Aunt Mable's arthritis, but that's my will, right? Help me out on this one."

"I would use a lifting-up prayer for Aunt Mable, something like this, 'Father, my aunt is in great discomfort with arthritis. I lift her up to Your mercy and compassion. Show her Your presence in her suffering and let her know that You will never leave her or forsake her. And if You would cure her arthritis, what a fantastic testimony that would be to You! In Jesus' name, amen.'"

The look on Jack's face reflected something like his suddenly discovering that he had one foot in heaven.

"You've given me a whole new look at prayer. I'm starting to see how I can pray continually without being bored out of my mind or saying the same stuff over and over." His voice bubbled over with enthusiasm.

They talked several more minutes about our daily bread and how God provides us with all we need, both physical and spiritual, especially the spiritual. Jack kept his pen moving.

Manny pressed on to the next petition. "Jack, we've covered the daily bread pretty well. Let's take a look at *Forgive us our trespasses as we forgive those who trespass against us.*

"This doesn't mean we keep confessing the same sins over and over. We confess what we've done or not done of late. It may be losing your temper with your wife or boys, or not reading the Bible for two days. It could be your having 'just one little drink' at the company Christmas party with your co-workers. Or missing a Bible study because you slept in on a Saturday morning.

"But it's more than just saying you're sorry for doing or not doing something. It's repenting of what you've done, which means promising not to do it again. Remorse is one thing; repentance is something else entirely.

"For example, your having a wee small drink, as the Irish would say, is dangerous for you because of your drinking problem, not because it's a bad thing in and of itself. If you do have that drink, don't beat yourself up or let Satan accuse you of being a loser. Repent and draw another line in the sand that you'll never drink again. And acknowledge to God that you don't want to lose His presence or your family. Remember it's a process. If you do cross a line, hopefully you don't draw a new line and cross it the next day. The distance between lines should be getting greater and greater until you no longer cross them."

Jack meant to ask about drawing and crossing and redrawing lines but didn't. It would have been a distraction from the main lesson. Besides, there would be a better time for this discussion in the future, when Jack would need it much more than he did right there. Jack, of course, had no idea when that would be or under what circumstances; Manny knew both.

"I think forgiving others is self-explanatory, right?"

Jack nodded.

"We're now at the last board—*And lead us not into temptation but deliver us from evil.*" Manny paused because he saw that Jack had something to say.

"I get the deliver us from evil, but why would God lead us into temptation? I must be missing something," Jack said, with a new-found humbleness.

Manny answered, "It's not that you're asking God to not lead you into temptation, but rather you're asking Him to lead you in paths away from temptation. For you, Jack, that would mean asking God to lead you away from situations or people that would tempt you to drink. Let's end there. What do you think about praying continually now?"

Jack was like a little boy or girl whose loving father pushes them on a 14-inch kid's bike until they have the skill and confidence to ride it on their own.

"It makes sense to me now, the how to pray continually. I expect I'll get a better feel for it with practice."

Jack had just stated one of the most important maxims of life in developing a skill to its greatest level—*practice makes perfect.* Indeed, the little boy gets over his shakiness in riding a bicycle after a few weeks, becomes rather proficient (as a little boy, that is) in a year, and twenty years later wins the Tour de France—a grueling race of three weeks that crowns the best bicycle rider in the world—because of years and years of daily practice, pushing himself to the utmost to achieve the highest.

Manny didn't expect Jack to win the Tour de France of prayer, but he wanted to encourage him to have more than a passing interest in continual prayer.

"Yes, Jack," he said, "you *will* get better with practice if you stick to it. And you'll draw ever so much closer to Jesus through continual prayer. If you'll remember from the chart I showed you on the plane trip to Chicago, that's where you'll find the safety you're longing for."

Jack looked up from his note taking.

"That's a good reminder for me. It *is* the safest place on earth I've been searching to find, and if continual prayer will keep me there, that's what I'm going to do."

As are most alcoholics, Jack was good at making promises but not so good at carrying them out. God's plan for Jack included having an intimate relationship with him through Scripture and prayer. It did not include abusing alcohol. When God's plan and Jack's plan became the same plan, that would be the day Jack would rest secure in the safest place on earth.

Had that day finally arrived with the conclusion of this eighth lesson? Jack convinced himself it had. He did, however, have one more question for Manny.

"I think I have down praying the Lord's Prayer as an outline of prayer and will keep practicing it until it becomes second nature to me. You've also shown me how to pray Scripture. Could you give a couple other suggestions to help me pray continually."

"Of course," Manny answered. "Everything you do during the day can turn you to prayer and everything you see happening around you and all the people in your life, and ..."

Manny suddenly stopped his enumeration of all the things Jack could pray for during the day. He could have continued on for an hour, but there wasn't the time.

"I could go on and on, Jack, but let me simplify it—you can pray at every turn of the day, when you go from doing one thing to doing another, from the time you brush your teeth in the morning to the time you turn off the lights at night. Does that make sense?"

"It does," Jack responded, "but I meant more things like the Lord's Prayer that I could use as an outline."

Manny was prepared for that question and pulled out a note card and handed it to Jack.

"Here's a note card for you that lists the Lord's Prayer and some other sources of prayer. That will be a start for you, and you'll find other sources if you seek them out."

Sources of Prayer

The Lord's Prayer

The 23rd Psalm

The 8 Beatitudes: Matt. 5:3-10

Psalms and Proverbs

Specific Prayers in the Bible

Jack put the note card into the inside pocket of his suit coat and left St. James with joy in his heart and a bounce in his step.

The card ended up in the trash of a dry cleaners three weeks later when a clothes sorter removed it prior to putting the jacket into a large drum machine filled with solvent.

Praying the Lord's prayer as an outline was energizing for a month; then it became less so. Jack could handle the discipline of reading the Bible twice a day and praying through the Lord's prayer framework at least once a day, but praying at every turn took more will power than he could muster. His mind bounced back and forth between what he had to do for work, all the distractions of the day, and an endless news cycle that he followed on his smartphone.

Eight Months Later

Jack lived in a relatively safe place spiritually and phys-ically for the next eight months. If someone were making a list of what active committed Christians should be doing with their lives, Jack would show up somewhere on that list. Maybe not the first entry, but not too far down.

He read the Bible twice a day, like Manny had instructed him. That pattern became an ingrained habit, like breathing in and breathing out. He returned to his Bible study group on Saturday mornings and agreed to their goal of memorizing seventy Bible verses, using a technique and content developed by the Navigator's ministry. That led him to a habit of praying ten different verses a day for every day of the week, which he incorporated into his daily exercise runs instead of listening to music. Jack was good at following routines, but following Jesus is more than simply a routine.

He became employee-of-the-year at his company and de-veloped into a recognized leader in the church he and his fami-ly had joined. A nominating committee asked him to become an elder, and he accepted. Jack felt he had turned his life around 180 degrees and felt content with what he had accomplished. His mind didn't grasp that one is either growing in faith or de-clining, no matter how much or how little. There's no plateau, no standing pat, no inn at the end of the road.

The more Jack became self-assured, self-contented, self-pleased and self-possessed, his prayer life and Bible study went from passionate to uninspired to dreary and finally to pretend-ing he was a Christian. On the chart Manny had showed him at their fifth meeting, Jack had meandered from *Closer to Je-sus* to somewhere in the middle of the chart and then picked up speed as he headed toward the bar of the *Fallen World*.

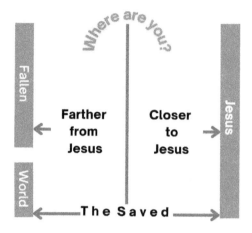

And the farther he meandered, the less he recognized it. When he started picking up speed away from Jesus, he had no awareness of his state of spiritual being. He moved from safety to danger and had no recognition of the journey. Whatever Christian activity he participated in, it was more duty than anything else. He did what his Christian friends expected him to do, nothing more and very much less. When they praised his devotion to Christ, it reinforced his belief that he was a dutiful Christian.

He thought fondly of Manny every now and again but less and less as time went on. He believed he no longer needed him. He felt he was now his own man, a solid citizen and Christian who was secure and comfortable with his own self.

"I'm not the person I once was," he thought. "Finally, I'm a card-carrying, respected member of society." He laughed as he said aloud to the fireplace, "I'm healthy, wealthy, and wise. I've arrived at the station where God wants me."

It would have been a blessing if a small bolt of lightning would have struck him when he said that, not enough to kill him but enough to jolt him into rethinking his station in life. He was, in fact, the living embodiment of Proverbs 16:18—"Pride goes before destruction, a haughty spirit before a fall."

On a Labor Day afternoon, four couples from church met at a restaurant in the suburbs. Three of the couples ordered a glass of wine before dinner and told the waiter he didn't have to bother asking if they wanted another later. "We are one and done," they said.

Jack laughed and declared, "I'll have one and done as well."

He made his decision in the blink of an eye, with no pause for reflection, as if he'd been asked to say grace before the meal. Marianne had a look of concern on her face but didn't say anything. She stayed with water.

Three weeks later, Jack was at a bar with high-school friends for a meal before attending a college football game. Marianne accompanied him. They were all drinking, not heavily, but more than one drink. He had been successful with one glass of wine a few weeks ago, and this time went blink-blink and had two glasses of wine. Then the wheels of his sobriety came off. He had three beers at the game and told Marianne to shut up when she protested the second beer. She had to drive home—in chilly silence.

From the day of the football game, Jack's drinking evolved quickly into out-of-control. Wine and beer gave way to strong mixed drinks and then to whiskey—straight. A liter would last two days at most, sometimes less. Long bouts at bars with rowdy friends became the weekend norm. He was the life of the party to the heavy drinkers, buying round after round, as they toasted their hero. The bar tabs were staggering. He stopped reading the Bible. He stopped praying the 70 Scripture verses because he stopped his daily run routine, and he abandoned any other prayers.

When confronted with rumors about his drinking by his church, he resigned from the elder board. They had no right to judge him. His company didn't want to fire him for dereliction of his work duties. Instead, they put him on a three-month leave of absence at half pay and told him he could have his job back when he turned his life around. They suggested he go to a rehab facility to dry out. He didn't do that.

After being stopped by the highway patrol and charged with a DUI, his wife asked him to leave, with tears in her eyes but resolve in her heart. The two boys watched him pack his bags and stared at him with wondering eyes as he walked out the door.

Jack's accommodations became seedier and seedier because he was spending all his money on alcohol for himself and his drinking buddies. His road to ruination accelerated steadily and steeply downward until finally reaching the bottom on a Friday night. Three policemen arrested him for being drunk and disorderly in a bar known for such conduct, but not on the scale he exhibited that night.

When morning dawned and Jack sobered up, he cried the tears of a broken man. "Where do I go from here?" he wondered. "What's to become of me? I've lost everything. I'm no good to anyone." Thoughts of ending his life crept into his mind. The final solution to all his problems.

He lifted his head from his hands when he heard a key in the door of his cell. "You've had bail posted for you," the jailer said.

"Who would post bail for me?" Jack asked the jailer. "I don't have a friend in the world. Even my own family has disowned me."

"I dunno," answered the man who held the door open for him, "but he's waiting for you down at the booking counter."

Jack shuffled uneasily to the door leading to the lobby of the jail and recognized the person who had bailed him out. He was tall and sturdy, with large hands and an oval face, and dressed in blue slacks and a red sweater.

"Hello, Jack," Manny said. "I thought it might be a good time for me to show up in your life again." He handed Jack a bundle of clothes and a shaving kit. "The guard here will show you a room where you can shower, shave, and make yourself presentable. I'll wait out here."

Thirty minutes later, Jack emerged with clean hair, shaved face, new khaki pants, a white shirt, and a pullover blue sweater. He was clean on the outside but polluted on the inside.

"Welcome to the world of the living," Manny said, and led him out to a waiting taxi. "Just drive around wherever you want," he said to the cab driver. "My friend and I have much to talk about."

For two miles, Manny looked at Jack with those piercing eyes and said nothing. Jack's great shame kept him from saying anything, until he finally realized he was the one who had to start the conversation.

"You must really be disappointed in me," Jack said.

"Why do you say that?" Manny answered. A five-word question fit his plan to let Jack do the talking for now. His turn would come later.

"Because I forgot everything you taught me. Because I went back to drinking and going my own way. And I stopped reading the Bible and praying. Worst of all, I stopped following Jesus." Jack put his head in his hands and started to weep. "Why do you even bother with me? I'm no good. I've fallen too far."

Manny spoke with great compassion and calm. "You're no worse than I thought you could be. You've not disappointed me, but you've caused me great sorrow. My heart cries for you. I haven't given up on you; please don't give up on yourself."

Jack sobbed even louder with Manny's words. "Where do I go from here, Manny?" That was the first time Jack had used Manny's name in talking with him. "How can God ever forgive me for abandoning Him like I did?"

"Oh, Jack, you need to learn so much more about who God really is, not who you think He is. God is the God of a thousand chances. He never gives up on you. He always forgives you when you repent. You can start anew at any time."

"How, Manny? How can I start anew? My life is such a mess, I don't know where to start."

"Let's start here," Manny said.

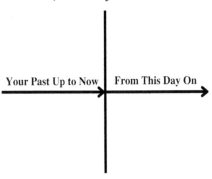

He took his electronic tablet out of the briefcase he had brought with him in the taxi and opened it to the sixth graphic, which pictured the concept he was about to introduce.

He passed it over to Jack.

"You can't change your past, Jack, but you don't have to let it define your future. You can draw a line in the sand and say, "From this day on, I will let God direct my life. I will go His way and not my way. I will follow Jesus wherever He goes. And then, my friend, you don't look back. You never look back."

Jack looked at the drawing. A light dawned in his mind, but there was darkness at the edges. "But what if I fall again, Manny? What if I go back to the old Jack again? Would I be lost forever then? I think I would; God's patience and grace must eventually run out for me."

Manny looked straight at Jack, as the cab drove down a narrow road with a picturesque lake on one side and a spectacular sports complex on the other. "I'm not going to burden you with theology here, Jack, other than to point out that we can lean on God's promise: 'Never will I leave you; never will I forsake you.' That's such an important promise that it's found in both the Old Testament in Deuteronomy and in the New Testament in Hebrews.

"Practically speaking, if you fall back again and repent again, you draw a new line in the sand. As many times as you truly repent, God will forgive your sins and take you back. He knows how difficult it is to break free from an addiction."

"So I can keep on sinning and keep on repenting?" Jack naively asked. "That doesn't seem right."

"The Apostle Paul was asked the same question back in his day, and this was his answer in the first two verses of Chapter 6 in his letter to the Romans.

> What shall we say then? Shall we continue
> in sin that grace may abound? Certainly not! How
> shall we who died to sin live any longer in it?

"What Paul is talking about here is a lifestyle of sin, not a single act or two of failure. Jesus died on the cross to take away your sinful nature. That means you change from your natural inclination to sin to a spiritual inclination not to sin. If you decide to keep on sinning every chance you get, you are denying Jesus's sacrifice for you. You are rejecting His salvation and resurrection. Again, I don't want to get into the theology of what that means, other than to say you don't want to go there.

"Whatever you do, you do for the honor of God. That doesn't include drinking yourself into a stupor or throwing your family on an ash heap. That, in fact, can be a guideline for decisions in your life: 'Does what I'm about to do honor God?'

"Does that mean you will never fall short again? Absolutely not! But it does mean you will not seek out sin. God knows you are frail and subject to temptation. He does not condemn you for your failures, if you recognize them as such and repent and ask for His forgiveness.

"With time and resolve on your part, any lines you draw in the future will hopefully be farther and farther apart, until one day a line you draw will be the last line. You must hate sin and want to live a life without it. You must have that attitude, that resolve. That's what God wants. When you draw your line in the sand today, you must intend that it will be the last line you draw. Does that make sense, Jack?"

Manny provided the lightning bolt Jack needed back when he thought he was the Christian God wanted him to be. He hadn't understood then that Christianity is not what you do but who you are in Christ.

"That was really a stupid question I asked, wasn't it Manny? I understand your answer. I want to draw that line in the sand right now, right where I'm sitting. I want to start over again, and I want this to be the last line I draw. It's kind of like being born-again again, if that's possible."

"It *is* possible, Jack. You don't need to be saved again, but you can be born-again into a new relationship with Jesus Christ based on a deeper knowledge of Him and what He did for you. Indeed, you can become born-again again."

Jack was glad he could start over again and what that might mean for his spiritual life, his family and his job. But he also had a healthy fear that he might not be able to pull it off.

"You're going to help me straighten out my life with God

and my family and all, right Manny? Can we start now and drive around for another hour?"

"You asked me two questions, Jack. The answer to the first one is yes, I will help you reconcile with God and your family and slip back into your job. The answer to the second one is no, we are not going to start right now. You need to build a solid spiritual foundation before we embark on transforming the old fallen Jack into the new spiritually awake Jack."

"And how is that going to happen?" Jack asked.

He felt uneasy with needing to prepare instead of starting to reclaim his life in the next minute. His thought about transforming his own life was an immediate red flag and a disqualifier to the process of transformation. He didn't have what it takes to start over again; he never did. Willpower alone to follow one step behind Jesus wasn't good enough; it often isn't. A passion to succeed and boundless enthusiasm to be born-again again wouldn't carry the day.

Then a thought flashed into his mind. The fear that he might not be able to pull off this transformation became more than a fear. It became a certainty that he couldn't remake himself by his own willpower. He knew that now as if it were written in his mind with indelible ink. It may seem like a small thing—that thought—but it's probably the most important realization an addict can come to.

"There's a four-day men's retreat put on by Adult and Teen Challenge at that hotel." Manny pointed out the window to a conference hotel they were passing at exactly that moment. "I've registered you for it. It starts this Thursday morning at 8 a.m. and runs through Sunday evening. The retreat's theme is God's Way to Break Your Addictions. There will be nearly two hundred Christian men there who are struggling with alcohol and drug addictions. They've tried to break their habits on their own too many times to remember. You'll learn much about them, yourself, and how to hitch a ride in a vehicle you won't be driving."

"I'll be there," Jack responded, without hesitation. "Anything else?"

"You know me well, Jack. There's always something else.

First of all, I want you to ponder alcohol."

"Ponder what about alcohol?" Jack asked. Jack knew what ponder meant but pondering alcohol seemed like a strange assignment. After all, wasn't that his problem—thinking about drinking all the time.

"Ask the Holy Spirit," was Manny's response.

Jack looked at Manny with meekness and respect. He had learned not to question his wisdom or foretelling. "When will we meet again, Manny?"

"When you're ready Jack." They had circled a radius of five blocks and were back at the retreat hotel. "I've paid for the upcoming retreat for you, Jack, and booked a room you can check into today and stay in until the retreat ends."

"How can I ever repay you, Manny?" Jack asked, which was a rather foolish question.

Manny answered with two words, "You can't."

The cab driver opened the door for Jack and departed to who knows where with Manny in the back seat. When Jack entered his room, he found a closet filled with new clothes, a bureau filled with socks and underwear and other necessities, and a prepaid credit card of $2,000 on the top of a desk. The retreat would start in three days.

After the Conference

The actual name of the retreat was *Does Jesus Really Care?*
A man with a deep sonorous voice started the opening session
by reading the passage of Jesus calming a storm, found in
Mark 4:35-41.

> That day when evening came, he said to his
> disciples, "Let us go over to the other side." Leav-
> ing the crowd behind, they took him along, just as
> he was, in the boat. There were also other boats with
> him. A furious squall came up, and the waves broke
> over the boat, so that it was nearly swamped. Jesus
> was in the stern, sleeping on a cushion. The disciples
> woke him and said to him, "Teacher, don't you care if
> we drown?"
>
> He got up, rebuked the wind and said to the
> waves, "Quiet! Be still!" Then the wind died down
> and it was completely calm.
>
> He said to his disciples, "Why are you so afraid?
> Do you still have no faith?"
>
> They were terrified and asked each other, "Who
> is this? Even the wind and the waves obey him!"

The reader left the stage to the right, and a highly noted
pastor from California entered from the left and stepped up to
the podium. He straightened his tie and smoothed out his suit-
coat before addressing those in attendance. "Men, those disciples were frightened by the fierce storm and thought they were
in the most dangerous place on earth. Their boat was about to
be swamped, and they were about to be drowned. In actuality,
they were in the safest place on earth—in the boat with Jesus.

"You men have been battling your addictions, some of
you for many years. You have prayed and prayed for Jesus
to keep you from drowning in alcohol or drugs. You may have

even muttered, 'God, don't You hear my prayers to take away my addiction? Don't You care about me?'

"Let it sink in, men? The safest place you can possibly be is where Jesus is, just like the disciples in the boat.

"Jesus really does care about you and will protect you—if you give up your own striving and trust in Him. Face it, you haven't done a good job of staying sober by vowing to never drink or use drugs again. You say no-no-no to using, being around others who use, and spending time in low places. If that had worked, you wouldn't be here today.

"You've been looking at staying safely sober from your point of view. When this conference concludes, I pray you'll come to realize that it's God's perspective that's crucial, not yours. I'm going to read three Bible passages that will underscore the theme of this conference. The first is Isaiah 41:10.

> So do not fear, for I am with you;
>   do not be dismayed, for I am your God.
> I will strengthen you and help you;
>   I will uphold you with my righteous right
> hand.

"The second is Isaiah 46:4

> Even to your old age and gray hairs
>   I am He, I am He who will sustain you.
> I have made you and I will carry you;
>   I will sustain you and I will rescue you.

"And the third is Jeremiah 29:11-13."

> "For I know the plans I have for you," declares the LORD, "plans to prosper you and not to harm you, plans to give you hope and a future. Then you will call on me and come and pray to me, and I will listen to you. You will seek me and find me when you seek me with all your heart."

For four days, Jack soaked in the message that he couldn't stay sober under his own power. He could only turn his life around by turning to Jesus and letting Him lead, like a dance partner with two left feet swirling confidently around the dance floor in the arms of a dancer from heaven.

By the end of the conference, Jack felt like he'd been given a ticket to a lifetime of sobriety. All he had to do was stop depending on himself and start trusting in Jesus alone to keep him safe from dangerous places and sinful activities. He knew his own willpower was not to be trusted. Throughout the day, he would say over and over again, "Not my will but Thine be done."

Early on the morning of the last day, while he was in deep prayer and meditation, he authored a poem that he immediately realized came from the Holy Spirit and not himself.

You are the song in me today,
With all I think and all I say,
With all events that come my way.

Your melody my spirit plays;
I'll tune within and humbly praise
Your presence in me all my days.

It's not what I achieve for You;
I'll strive no more in all I do.
It's only what You do through me;
I'll wait for You on bended knee.

Jack vowed he would carry Jesus along with him wherever he went, listen to His guidance, and trust Him with all his heart. He thought to himself, "There are no more decisions for me to make, only instructions from Him to follow. How much more simple could it be?"

He came to realize that instead of saying no to using, he'd say yes to being near Jesus at all times. He was convinced that was the winning formula. Jack felt he truly could carry out his conviction to stay with Jesus, like the disciples in the boat on the stormy sea. He was certain he'd never drink again, with all his heart and with all his soul and with all his mind and with all his strength. He looked in the mirror in the background and addressed himself, "This time I'll make it because

I'm now wearing the armor of God and not my own clothes. I promise you, Jesus, that I'll stay right next to You to the ends of the earth." He looked in the mirror and said, "I promise you, Jack, that my addiction is in the rear view mirror, not because of anything I can do but because of what Jesus will do through me."

For alcohol and drug addicts, there are hundreds of promises made and hundreds of promises broken, like a grave-yard of broken tombstones. Would this time have a different outcome? With everything that happened in the conference, it seemed that something new was in the wind. Jack had new knowledge, new understandings, and faith that it would be different this time. He was no longer the hopeless drunk Jack. He was a beloved child of God who would be protected by Him, now and forever, amen.

Lesson Nine

The day after the retreat was a spring-like day at the end of March. Jack walked a couple of miles to his favorite running route—a lake that was almost perfectly round and exactly three miles in circumference. He felt good enough to start running as soon as he reached the path that circled the lake, but his shape and endurance had suffered significantly during the last half year. He ran for a bit, then walked for a bit, and followed that pattern until he reached the half-way point, which was a small park with a few picnic tables and a couple of charcoal grills. He noticed something lying on the farthest picnic table, but couldn't quite make out what it was for all his huffing and puffing.

One block later, he slowed down to a walk. One block after that, he heard steps behind him and turned around to see a man about six feet tall with a sturdy athletic build and a broad chest, wearing a crimson red running outfit. Jack stopped and let Manny catch up to him.

"You're walking in the wrong direction," were the first words Manny spoke to him, not "How are you doing?" or "Good to see you."

Jack smiled broadly when he saw Manny and spoke with great enthusiasm. "That retreat you signed me up for was fantastic, miles beyond my expectations. I don't think I'll ever be the same again. It's gonna be me and Jesus for the rest of my days, guaranteed." Jack started to say more about the conference and his transformation, but Manny interrupted him.

"You're standing in the wrong place, Jack, and you're going in the wrong direction. You've been going clockwise around this lake, following the direction of the arrows the park people put in, just like most everyone else. You need to turn around

180 degrees and go in the opposite direction. It's symbolic, Jack. When the world goes in one direction, you need to go the opposite way."

Jack didn't have a clue what Manny meant, but turn around he did and followed him back to the picnic area. Manny led him to the farthest picnic table and sat down on the side with the briefcase Jack had seen five minutes ago as he ran by.

As was his custom, Manny waited for Jack to initiate the conversation. "What do you mean about my going in the wrong direction, Manny?" Jack asked. "And my standing in the wrong place? You've totally lost me."

"I know I have, Jack. I'm glad the retreat went so well for you, but your vow to carry Jesus along with you wherever you go and your statement to me that it's going to be you and Jesus from here on out is precisely upside down and 180 degrees in the wrong direction."

Jack knew better than to say anything or ask anything, plus he didn't have a clue as to what Manny was referring to.

Manny took the electronic notebook out of his briefcase and showed Jack a seventh graphic he had sketched that morning, again not intending it to hang in an art museum.

"Did you disown Jesus before you had that glass of wine last September?" Manny asked Jack.

Jack answered with a simple, "No."

"So it was still you and Jesus then?"

"Yes."

"And did you abandon Jesus before and during the football game when you abandoned your sobriety?"

"No."

"How about the last six months when you and alcohol were best friends? Did you sever your relationship with Jesus?"

Jack was perplexed with Manny's line of questioning. Where was he going and what was the sketch all about? "I still went to church on Sundays and asked Jesus about a thousand times to stop my drinking. I did not disown Him. I did not abandon Him. He remained my friend ..." At that point Jack hesitated before finishing the sentence. "... but at a distance, I guess. I prayed and prayed, but He stayed away. I figured He'd given up on me."

Manny gave Jack that look that went right through him. "Jesus will never give up on you, Jack. And He didn't move away from you. You moved away from Him. If it was you and Jesus then, and you have just vowed that it will be you and Jesus for the rest of your days, guaranteed, you've already proven that doesn't work."

"But this time will be different, Manny. That retreat changed my thinking and changed my life. I'll really follow through now. I know I will. I'm committed like never before."

"Jack," Manny said in a soft voice full of compassion, "you've had a mountaintop experience, which will last for a few months. I have no doubt you are sincere when you commit to a life of you and Jesus, but when you come back down off the mountain, eventually alcohol will come between you and Jesus, and you'll walk away from Him again. I've seen it happen a thousand times with other addicts that were convinced it would be different this time, guaranteed. The trouble is, they were standing in the wrong place, just like you are."

Jack looked at the two drawings, and the Holy Spirit clicked on a light bulb in his mind. "If I'm seeing this right, Manny, you're saying I've been putting myself first and Jesus second, and what I need to do instead is to put Jesus first and me below Him. Is that what you mean by my standing in the wrong place?"

"That's exactly what I mean, Jack. You've been treating Jesus like a puppy dog, asking Him to follow you and protect you. Then, when you find something else you want more, like alcohol, you drift in that direction. It will always be that way until you stop asking Jesus to follow you and make the choice that you will follow Him for the rest of your days. You need to stand in the position of the second heart, not the first. The point you missed in the passage in Mark about Jesus calming the storm is this. The disciples didn't start bailing water out of the boat and ask Jesus to help them keep from being swamped and going to the bottom of the Sea of Galilee. That wouldn't have worked. The storm was too fierce. They woke Jesus up and cried for help. It was all they could do, and He calmed the storm.

"That's the way it needs to be with you, Jack. If you think you're in charge of your life and all you need is for Jesus to help you every now and again, like a person you've hired for the job, then you will fail again and again, and end your life as a hopeless drunk."

Those were strong words, but spoken in love. "But if you apprentice yourself to Jesus and follow Him where He goes, you'll be safe. In fact that's the safest place you can be in this world. There will be storms and troubling times, but you're safe if you stick by him, if you let Him be before you, not alongside you. Jesus is not your buddy. He's your Lord and Master.

"Listen to these four verses from Psalm 73, which amplifies the point." Manny didn't open any Bible.

Yet I am always with You;
You hold me by my right hand.
You guide me with Your counsel,
and afterward You will take me into glory.
Whom have I in heaven but You?
And earth has nothing I desire besides You.
My flesh and my heart may fail,
but God is the strength of my heart
and my portion forever.

"Notice what the psalmist says in the first two lines, Jack. It's a given that you've been with God since the day you were born-again. But notice that you don't hold Him with your right hand: He holds you. The question is whether you let Him take hold of your right hand and guide you with His counsel.

"There was a book written years back called *GOD IS MY CO-PILOT*. That's a terrible concept. If God is your co-pilot, you're sitting in the wrong seat. You need to let God be your pilot. He's the one who flies the airplane.

"That's what my sketch is all about. You've been living your life upside-down. You've been asking Jesus to be along for your ride. That's why you've had so much trouble. You really need to let Jesus be the King in your life, and you're along for His ride."

Jack had been busy listening and taking notes. Three minutes passed while Jack finished writing. Then he looked up at Manny, who was silhouetted against the shimmering lake behind him. "I don't know what to say, Manny. I can see I've been living my life upside-down, but how this sketch will change my life, I don't know. It's a whole new way of looking at my walk with Jesus. I thought I was squared away after the retreat, but I was only paddling in the shallows. This is a life changer. I mean I ...."

Jack's voice trailed off. It's like he'd parachuted out of an airplane for the first time and landed on his feet.

"You need time to ponder this, Jack," Manny said. "Do you remember when I asked you last time to ponder alcohol?"

"Yes," Jack answered.

"You didn't do that, did you?"

"I tried but came up empty," Jack answered.

"I know you did. But now I want you to ponder it again, given the new understanding you have from the *Jesus and you* sketch. This time you'll get it."

"When should we meet again, Manny?" Jack asked.

"When you've had time to think about today and are able to see your relationship with God through a new filter."

"What does that mean? A new filter."

"Well," laughed Manny, "that will give you another thing to ponder before we meet."

Manny stood up from the picnic table and walked off counterclockwise on the path along the lake. Jack watched him disappear into a row of trees as the path turned north.

Lesson Ten

Jack stayed in the retreat hotel for three more days and three more nights. He spent hours on his knees and hours reading the Bible at the desk in his room. He read the 4th chapter in Mark over and over again. And he read the entire Gospel of John, which Manny had assigned to him.

At one point, he wrote this prayer in the journal he kept for recording insights the Holy Spirit gave him.

> The battle in my heart can only be won through Christ's work within me, remaking my desires, rewiring my mind, and renewing my heart. It's hard to put Jesus first. I desire to hide God's truth in my soul, but the world and my interaction with it want to be first instead.
>
> Christ, who loved me first, will also help me put Him first thing in my day, my thinking, and my life.

"Yes," Jack thought, "It's like Manny showed me. I keep wanting to put myself and the world first. My battle is with alcohol, and it can only be won by Christ's work within me, not by anything I do. But even putting Christ first is not within my reach. Only the Spirit of Christ can achieve that in me."

Jack had arrived at a critical concept, but he didn't realize how urgently important it was. It became a trace in his mind instead of a deep fissure, amidst other traces. It's like a baseball pitcher who discovers a new technique, in the middle of a game, to put more spin on a curve, but then doesn't incorporate it into his daily practice and never masters it.

He also found a prayer by St. Augustine as he searched on his computer for saints who could offer spiritual insights.

And see, You were within,
and I was in the external world
and sought You there,
and in my unlovely state
I plunged into those lovely created things
which You made.
You were with me,
but I was not with You.

"This also fits into what Manny told me. Jesus is always with me because I accepted Him as my Savior. To my deprivation, I'm not always with Him. That's my problem."

At the end of the third day, Jack had pondered the word alcohol, had meditated on it, and had asked the Holy Spirit to reveal to him what alcohol was in his life. The Holy Spirit led him to read the third chapter of Genesis over and over and over again. He didn't know why. As he stilled his mind of his own thoughts, a 40 watt light bulb came on in his mind. He turned to his notes with Manny and his eyes lit on the second graphic he had shown him.

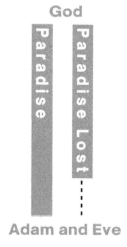

The light bulb increased to 100 watts, and now he could clearly see what alcohol was in his life. When Adam and Eve went their own way, they became separated from God and the safe life they had, and they plunged into dangerous possibilities around every corner. His drinking distanced him from God and plunged him into dangerous possibilities. Then he looked at the third graphic ...

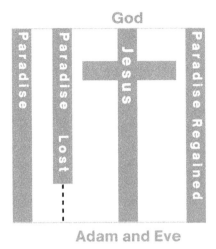

... and the light bulb in his mind dropped to sixty watts. If he was saved, then he wasn't separated from God, but yet it seemed like he was. Then he looked at the fourth graphic and the light bulb shone brightly at 150 watts.

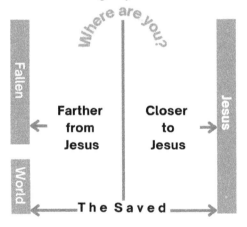

When he used alcohol, he was not totally separated from God but enough so that he fit into the last two lines of St. Augustine's prayer.

> You were with me,
> but I was not with You.

That is, the farther he drifted toward the *Fallen World*-broken bar, the more distant he was from Jesus. Jesus was still with him, but he wasn't with Jesus. At that distance, he was on his own when it came to drinking or not drinking, and he further separated himself from the help he desperately needed. So drinking became the great distancer from God, an ill-fated substitute for Him (an idol), and a battle that couldn't be won on his own.

Jack also thought about what a new filter meant. "Let's see," he pondered, "a new filter is needed when an old filter gets dirty." With that thought, no light bulb, even of very low wattage, came on in his mind. Then he thought about different colored filters. "Let's see," he thought, "what if I'm seeing my relationship with God through a dark gray filter and decide to change to a bright blue filter?"

As he pondered that thought, a 20 watt bulb came on in his mind. "But what would the blue filter be?" That's as far as he could get. No answer was forthcoming. He needed Manny to illuminate that concept.

On the morning of the fourth day, as Jack was deep in prayer, he asked, "I want to follow You, Lord, instead of asking You to follow me. What is it You want me to do?" That was progress and the harbinger of the new filter. He became silent and waited for a response; it was the first time he had done that in his prayers—listening for God instead of being caught up in his own thoughts and asking God to bless them.

Somewhere from deep within him, he knew not where, Jack became aware of a whisper that was not audible but within reach, nevertheless.

"I am not so much interested in what you do as in who you are."

It took him by surprise. He had not been close enough in the past to hear from the Lord. He knew one thing for sure. Those words did not come from his own thoughts; they were like a foreign language to him. But as to what they meant, he had no idea. They may as well have been in Greek. His emotions were aflame with the importance of the words. He felt smitten. He rolled the words through his mind without further enlightenment or revelation. His will wanted to act on the strange sentence, but no direction appeared as to what that might be.

Jack became restless in his hotel room and decided to head out for a walk. Once on the street, he started walking northeast, like there was a little map in his head telling him to go that way. Ten minutes later he was at the Stone Arch Bridge that crosses the Mississippi River for a span of 2,100 feet, nearly a half mile. In another ten minutes, he was half-way across, and what he saw was spectacular. The view of the mighty Mississippi was breathtaking, with the Upper St. Anthony Falls to the northwest and the Lower St. Anthony Falls to the southeast. But Jack saw something else from where he was standing—the beauty and wonder of God's creation. He sensed that the Holy Spirit was in the Mississippi River but couldn't articulate that feeling into words.

"Hello, Jack," said a voice behind him. "How do you see the world from where you're standing?"

A rather odd way to start a conversation, thought Jack, as he gathered his thoughts from the east and the west to answer Manny's question.

"I see the world will flow more smoothly for me now, like the river I'm looking at. There have been falls in my life, like the two I'm looking at, but then the Mississippi flows smoothly on after that. I believe it will be the same with my life. I've come to some really significant realizations from reviewing and pondering the first four graphics you showed me. I think those realizations will be game changers for me."

Manny said one word in response—"Hmm." He was not impressed with Jack's answer. "And how do you think God sees this scene? Jack."

"I don't know," Jack answered. To Jack's way of thinking, Manny often asked questions that mystified him.

"I didn't think you would. You've been struggling with the concept of a new filter."

"I have been," Jack admitted. He was about to relate to Manny his thoughts on a new filter, when Manny raised his hand to silence him.

"Let me tell you what a new filter means for you. You've been seeing the world from your perspective, and that's caused you to make some dangerous and harmful decisions. A new filter for you would be to see everything from God's viewpoint. For example, standing here you're experiencing the first chapter of Genesis, when God separated the land from the water." Jack hadn't thought of that.

"And in the second chapter of Genesis, God created Adam and Eve, of whom you are a descendant. And in the third chapter, Adam and Eve separated themselves from God when they chose to listen to Satan instead of Him. They went their own way instead of listening to God, and you've done the same thing with your drinking and your other self-centered activities. So, I would say that God is looking at you looking at the Mississippi River and wondering when you will immerse yourself in His life and experience His peace. He's been waiting patiently for you, Jack, to lean back on Jesus' breast, as the Apostle John did at the Last Supper. That's the safest place you can be, leaning so close to Jesus that you touch Him."

Jack needed a precise and clear assessment of the faulty filter with which he looked at the world and his life, and Manny gave it to him straight out. All Jack could do is bow his head and say, "You're right, Manny. I see it now. I need to see everything the way God sees it. That's the new filter."

Some people receive a slap on the face and become resentful. Others recognize it as tough love and become humble as they face the truth about themselves. Jack fell into the latter category.

There was no transition between the filter discussion and the upcoming alcohol discussion. "Tell me, Jack, what you learned by pondering alcohol?" Manny asked.

"I learned that anything that separates me from God is sin. And that the farther I drift toward the natural world of Adam, the more distant I am from Jesus. Worse yet, the farther I drift the less I recognize it. Jesus is still with me, but I'm not with Him. And the more I'm not with Jesus, the more out of reach I am from the help I desperately need." Jack paused to collect his thoughts. "So drinking becomes the great separator from God, and a battle I can't win on my own."

"Ah," said Manny, "the great separator. Well put, Jack.

Very well put! That's exactly what alcohol is for you. Even for those who are not alcoholics, drinking beyond moderation becomes a separator from Jesus, an altered state of mind in which Jesus is nowhere to be found. Though it's a spiritual separator for a brief period of time for those who drink only on occasion, it can lead to damaging results in the natural world if a person leaves a party in a car and gets picked up for a DUI. Or says something that can never be taken back.

"Anything else of importance in your three-day retreat?"

The fact that he asked the question led Jack to believe that Manny knew there was something else. Jack stood by the rail of the bridge watching the river pass below him, not intending to say anything more, but then he did.

"I think I heard from the Lord this morning, Manny, but it wasn't with audible words. How does that work? How does anyone hear from God? Did I really hear from Him or was it just my imagination?"

Manny lifted his head and turned to Jack. "That's a good question. Let me tell you how God speaks to us, and then you tell me if you think it was Him or your own imagination." Jack gestured with his head in agreement.

"If God is within you, it makes sense that He speaks to you. Your job is to listen and determine whether it's really of Him or of you."

"How do I do that?" Jack asked.

"The most important way is to ask yourself whether what you heard lines up with Scripture or not. If you think God is telling you to say something harsh to your wife, that doesn't line up. If you are hearing that you should talk to someone about Christ, that does line up.

"A second test is to determine if what you have heard is something you would not likely have said or even thought about. That's an indication that it's something beyond yourself. There are other tests and ways to confirm a word from God, but let's stick with these two for now.

"Now, as to how specifically God talks to anyone, it's important to understand that God is Spirit and He speaks to us by the power of His still, small voice speaking to our inner person.

Sometimes what we hear is word for word what God wants us to hear. More often, He plants thoughts into our minds that we express with our own words, based on our experiences, education, and personality. The same thoughts conveyed into someone else's mind would be expressed in different words.

"Put another way, God provides the thoughts and you contribute the words. It's an us thing. God speaks to us with the language of human beings and through the inner sanctum of our own mind. Language is just one of the mediums to express God's thoughts. An artist uses the realm of painting or sculpture to express impressions from the Lord. A musician, her music. Eric Liddle, portrayed in Chariots of Fire, said he ran to express God's pleasure.

"Why don't you tell me what you heard from the Lord, and we'll put it to the test."

What the Lord said to him was burned into Jack's mind, so he didn't need to check notes or bring them up front. "'I am not so much interested in what you do as in who you are,' were the exact words I heard."

Manny put his hand to his mouth and dropped down on one knee to the sidewalk.

"You have heard from the Lord directly," he said. "There can be no doubt about it. It lines up with Scripture from the first chapter of Genesis to the last chapter of Revelation and everywhere in between. You see, Jack, what you do comes out of who you are. Your alcohol addiction comes out of who you think you are. Once you change your filter to how God sees you and who He wants you to be, you will stop drinking. You would never have come up with this on your own. In fact, it's the complete opposite of how you've been seeing the world. For you it's been 'do, do' and God is telling you it's really 'be, be' that He's interested in."

There was a long period of time spent in silence, with both Jack and Manny standing at the edge of the rail looking into the Mississippi River. There was nothing more for either of them to say. After five minutes, Manny turned and continued to where the bridge came out on the other side of the river. Jack turned back to the side from which he had come.

The Next Year or So

Jack memorized the drawing Manny had showed him in the taxi cab just before he dropped him off for the Adult and Teen Challenge retreat. It became seared in his mind like a brand on the hide of a cow, which was an apt illustration, for Jack felt himself branded for Christ.

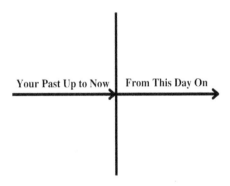

Jack desperately needed hope. Hope that he wasn't on his own in transforming his life from addiction to sobriety: Jesus was with him. Hope that he could start over right now and never look back on all his failures.

He looked fixedly at *From This Day On* with the eyes of an eagle. Normally, in deciding what action to take with such a challenge, he'd formulate in his mind how to proceed and ask God to bless his undertaking. Not this time. He asked the Holy Spirit what steps he should take and listened to the still, small voice of God that gave him three very specific directions.

1.   Commit with all your heart, mind, and will to follow Jesus.
2.   Make things right with your family.
3.   Get your job back.

With Step 1, the Holy Spirit laid Mathew 9:9 on Jack's heart.

> As Jesus went on from there, He saw a man named Matthew sitting at the tax collector's booth. "Follow Me," he told him, and Matthew got up and followed Him.

Jack substituted his own name in the verse to make it personal.

> Jesus saw a man named Jack sitting in front of a fireplace in the lower level of his home, and said, "Follow Me."

In his mind's eye, Jack saw himself getting up from the couch in front of the fireplace and following Jesus.

Then the Spirit led him to a song that resonated in him, like the strings in a piano respond to the vibrations of a tuning fork.

> I have decided to follow Jesus;
> I have decided to follow Jesus;
> I have decided to follow Jesus;
> No turning back, no turning back.

"Yes," Jack said to the prompting of the Holy Spirit, "I have decided to follow Jesus and there'll be no turning back. Wherever He leads, I will follow one step behind. I will trust Him for my sobriety, Him and no one else. I have faith that He is with me and will never leave me or forsake me. I will cling to Him like a little child clings to his mother."

As for Step 2, Jack called Marianne and asked if he could come back home sometime in the future, when she felt comfortable with it. When he told her about the retreat and his discussions with Manny and his commitment to follow Jesus, she said, "How about today? I'll set a plate for you at the dinner table." The two boys just about knocked him over with their exuberance over his return.

The third step came one week later. Jack met with the owner of his company and asked if he could have his job back because he had turned his life around, as requested. The owner didn't say, "Oh, sure, no problem. If you say you've turned your life around, that's good enough for me." Michael asked a flurry of questions, and Jack answered them as best he could. The final question was the clincher.

"And who's going to help you stay sober this time around, Jack? I'd suggested rehab for you and said the company would pay for it, but you didn't go in that direction. Why will this time be different?"

"Even if I'd gone to rehab, Michael, it would still be me trying to stay sober following their guidelines. I've talked to many addicts who have careened from one rehab facility to another and are still not sober long term. I can't do this on my own, even with professional help, if it's not faith based. I went to a retreat for addicts run by Adult and Teen Challenge. I have a Christian mentor who is an inspiration to me and whom I can call at any time. But most importantly, Michael, I'm anchoring my new life of sobriety on Jesus Christ. Instead of my asking Him to help me in my life, I've told Him I'll let him drive and I'll be the passenger. To sum it up, I've decided to follow Jesus."

With that final answer, Michael looked at Jack with the same piercing eyes that Manny employed, stood up and walked over to Jack, grabbed his hand with a firm shake, and said, "Done. See you next Monday."

Jack came to a realization about the Bible and Jesus that opened his eyes and led him to follow Jesus through long sessions of studying Scripture, like an athlete training for a decathlon. He already knew that the Bible was the Word of God about the Son. And the first verse of the Gospel of John told him that Jesus was the Word. Putting those two together meant that the exercise of studying the Bible was perhaps the most important training he could do to follow Jesus.

The Holy Spirit showed him that from the first book of Genesis to the last book of Revelation, the Bible is all about Jesus. On the stand next to the couch in front of the fireplace, Jack had a copy of *The Knowing Jesus Study Bible: A One-Year Study of Jesus in Every Book of the Bible*. He studied it first thing in the morning and last thing at night. It became like putting his clothes on in the morning to start the day and removing them at night to end the day.

Jack found in Matthew 18:20 that Jesus said, "Where two or three gather in My name, there am I with them." In his obedience to do what Jesus pointed to, Jack, joined a Saturday morning men's Bible study and was in a couples group Wednesday evenings with his wife, Marianne. In his mind and attitude, she became a spiritual partner in addition to being his wife. They prayed together every morning as a family before they went to work and the boys went to school, all four of them.

A large fireplace with a gas burner was embedded in the east wall of the lower level of Jack's home. For one hour each morning, before the sun came up, Jack sat on a couch in front of the fireplace studying the Bible, meditating on what he had just read, and praying on one verse or message that jumped out at him. Following that sequence, he read from a couple of daily devotionals. Some of the thoughts that came to him in meditation were observations that wouldn't knock your socks off, and some that were profound. He wrote the profound ones in a journal that he had started to keep some time back, at the suggestion of his pastor in an action-provoking sermon. He read one entry over and over because it had to do with following Jesus.

> Come near to God and He will come near to you. James 4:8

> It is not more knowledge that I need, Almighty God, but more seeking You here and there and everywhere.

> You are in the fireplace downstairs and in the office upstairs.

> You are in the kitchen where I eat
> And in the bedroom where I sleep.

> You are everywhere outside

And in every home, store, and building where
I set my foot.

Wherever I go, You are there first.

As Jack drew closer and closer to Jesus, the Holy Spirit
became more and more active in his life. One day, while driving from a business appointment in Philadelphia to another
such meeting in Baltimore, the Holy Spirit visited him with a
vision that was like a motion picture playing in his mind. This
is how he captured it in his journal.

> While driving to Baltimore last week, I envi-
> sioned a road of a much different nature running par-
> allel to the highway I was on.
>
> In a flash, I was walking on the other road, a
> path of smooth gravel, winding through woods and
> open spaces, with Christ ahead of me. He turned and
> spoke almost in a whisper, "Jack, come follow Me."
>
> I said, "Yes, Lord."
>
> He continued the conversation, "Do you see
> any need to pile up money for retirement?"
>
> I replied, "No, Lord."
>
> "Do you see any need for a new house, fashion-
> able clothes, or a shiny new car?"
>
> "No, my Lord."
>
> "Are there any needs you have on this road?"
>
> "None," I answered. "To be with You is all I
> want. You will provide everything I need." With this
> confession, I experienced a feeling of great peace.
>
> Alongside the road were wild animals and
> monsters, but I knew they couldn't harm me because
> I was with the King. As we were about to enter a
> dense woods, I had a strong urge to turn around and
> go back a few hundred yards.
>
> "Lord, I wish to see for just a minute what I
> have left behind." I returned to an opening in the
> woods and noticed the path I was on with Jesus stood
> above a deep ditch with steep sides. The ditch was
> filled with various distorted figures personifying
> greed, envy, gossip, pleasure, dishonesty, immorali-
> ty, alcoholism, and the other things of this world not
> part of the King's neighborhood. I also saw some real
> people, though I couldn't recognize anyone in partic-

ular.

"Come down with us," the misshapen figures and people shouted. "Life is good here. Don't be a Goody Two-Shoes. A life of pleasure is the best life of all. This is where you'll find happiness." But they didn't look happy, and a miry sludge lapped at their heels. I realized their lot in life was to slide back into that sludge, the whole dirty, tattered, and earthy lot of them. Yet, the ditch and what was in it tempted me.

Jesus showed up at that point and sighed, "Jack, come follow Me." Those in the ditch couldn't see Him. I realized if I crawled down into the ditch, I also would not be able to see Him. Eventually, I would forget Him, and the miry sludge would be lapping at my heels.

"Come, follow Me," Jesus repeated.

"Yes, Lord, I will follow You."

Those in the ditch heard the exchange and yelled, "You fool!" but they had no attraction for me anymore.

I was on the King's Highway with my Lord, and that's where I desired to be. Psalm 73:25 resonated in my mind: "Whom have I in heaven but You? And earth has nothing I desire besides You."

With that vision, Jack was certain that his battle with alcohol was over, in a similar manner to a college wrestler coming to realize that his opponent could never get the best of him, no matter what. Or a swimmer in a race looking over in the next lane to see his most powerful and determined opponent fading in the final stretch. His drinking was in the rear view mirror of his life. It was a book that had been closed and would never again be re-opened.

Was Jack really prepared to stay sober for a lifetime? He believed with all his heart that he was. The vision given him by the Holy Spirit convinced him. Following Jesus every step of the way was the end of the journey. It was a magical moment that all addicts search for—the Inn of Happiness and Peace and Sobriety at the end of a long and troubled road.

Oops

Six months later, Jack was in London to meet with the Renal Services medical staff of St. George's Hospital in the heart of the city. He showed them his company's state-of-the-art laser machine that reduced kidney stones to a fine dust. They had purchased equipment from Jack's company before, so it only took an hour of the afternoon before they inked an order.

As it so happened, that very evening a retirement party was being held for the retiring director of St. George's, who was widely respected and loved. Jack received a verbal invitation to represent his company and felt he couldn't refuse the offer. After all, that hospital was their largest customer in England and hadn't he just sold them a very pricey piece of medical equipment. He didn't think he needed to check with Michael because he knew this is what Michael would have done had he been there. He didn't think any further about it.

An army about to engage an enemy in battle first wants to know how large the other force is, exactly where they are located, what weapons they have, and where the danger zones will be as the fight progresses. They don't want to just show up on the battlefield and hope for the best. They want to be totally prepared.

Jack wasn't prepared for the enemy that would be at the retirement party nor what tactics he would use. Manny would have told Jack not to go, had he asked him. Michael would have instructed Jack to come up with a good reason not to go and pass on the invitation, but he was back in the States and didn't know anything about any retirement party.

The Lord's Prayer asks God to keep us away from temptation and the evil lurking in unforeseen places, but Jack didn't make that connection regarding the retirement party. To him, it wasn't really a big deal. After all, he felt he was protected from all temptations because he had been following Jesus so closely.

As Jack walked into the reception room of the very fancy and expensive restaurant in Covent Garden, he was immediately met by two men with trays of wine and other drinks. He hadn't anticipated that but handled it like a man who can see that a burner on a stove is hot and avoids touching it. Then Lizzie, the head of the Renal Services division, whom he had met with that afternoon, asked if he wanted her to get a mixed drink or beer or wine at a long bar against the back wall.

"How about just a Ginger Ale," he responded, and off she went. Jack had already found that he could have a good time without drinking, and though the temptation to imbibe was there, his commitment to stay sober won the battle. He avoided every temptation like a prize fighter who ducks the more lethal punches thrown at him and so avoids getting knocked out.

At 6 p.m. sharp, the master of ceremonies, who was the same person who had fetched the Ginger Ale for Jack, directed everyone to be seated. Lizzie turned to Jack, who stood seven feet from her, and surprised him.

"You'll be sitting at the head table with Dr. James, the retiring director. He requested you because your company has been such an integral part of our being on the leading edge of healthcare and medicine in so many of our departments. You've been a critical partner for us, and he wants to honor the company you represent, as well as Michael, your CEO. The two of them became close friends over the years, and he'd like you to fill in for him."

Jack felt the buttons popping off his shirt, metaphorically speaking, but didn't foresee the danger ahead. If he had, he could have prepared for it. Not only was he seated at the head table, but he ended up next to Dr. James, who occupied the center of the table, as the one being celebrated.

There were wine glasses filled halfway with Cava Champagne at every place at the head table and for every guest sitting at the smaller tables that filled the room. Jack had no intention of taking even a sip, but then he noticed that no one else was drinking from those glasses either. Instead, they were drinking whatever they had brought with them from the bar and kept going back to refill their glasses with more of the same.

He and Dr. James talked about the future of medical equipment in the next ten years. He'd have to relate the conversation to Michael when he got back home. Michael loved market research, and couldn't get enough of it from sources that he considered knowledgeable and credible. Dr. James fit neatly into both categories.

Just before the meal started to be served, Lizzie shushed the crowd and proposed a toast for Dr. James. That's what the Champagne glasses were for. Jack hadn't anticipated that. He'd never been to such a function before where he sat at the table of honor. Dr. James was asked to stand up, and everyone raised their glasses to toast him. Jack didn't know what to do, until Dr. James looked down at him and said, "Well, Jack, are you going to toast me or not?"

He felt like everyone in the room had their eyes riveted on him and the glass before him, still half full. In his imagination, he felt them all shouting at him, "Well, Jack, are you going to toast Dr. James or not?"

It would have been well for him to remember Galatians 1:10.

> Am I now trying to win the approval of human beings, or of God? Or am I trying to please people? If I were still trying to please people, I would not be a servant of Christ.

In the contest to please God or please people, the people won. In a moment of near panic, Jack downed the half-glass of Champagne in one gulp, just like all the guests did. In the snap of two fingers, a waiter filled his glass halfway up for the next toast.

The road to perdition starts with the first step. A person who commits adultery struggles with the first time; the second time becomes easier. So too, a young girl who steals from her mother is mortified with the initial theft, but with the wheels of rebellion oiled for the first time, her conscience weakens and the next thievery is much easier. It's a pattern of the natural world, and each subsequent transgression becomes less troublesome and more like tying your shoes.

So it was with Jack. Shouts of "toast, toast" filled the air every few minutes for an hour. There were ten toasts in all, and Jack was only too happy to discharge his duty for each one. After too much time had passed after the ninth toast, Jack himself proposed the last one. At that point, Jack was feeling high but not drunk enough to embarrass himself or his company by falling face-first into his crème brûlée.

Dr. James thanked Jack for coming to his retirement party. Lizzie shook his hand and wished him a good trip home in two days. The party goers scattered like birds escaping the cold for a warmer climate. They all had homes to go back to. Jack didn't, and the thought of going back to his hotel room at 7 p.m. was not appealing.

He had seen a pub on his way to the retirement party, about three blocks away. At the time, he had dismissed it as a thing of his past and felt sorry for the patrons he saw stumbling out the front door in various degrees of dishevelment.

"Maybe I'll just slip in for a nightcap," he considered in his mind. His will did not fight back. "There's no harm in that." With a chill in the air, the thought of a Black Russian cocktail warmed his body. "I can make one of those last an hour and get back to my hotel room by 9 p.m. and go to bed early."

With a spring in his step and gaiety in his heart, he arrived at the pub in ten minutes and went in convinced it would be a short visit of no consequence. Just killing some time. No warning sign was on the door and no one to tell him he was entering the most dangerous place for him in all of London. No Manny, no loving wife, no Holy Spirit, no Jesus living within him, not even a well-intentioned stranger. It was all Jack and what he wanted to do and to hell with the rest of them.

The Black Russian that would take an hour to nurse was drained in 30 minutes. The next one took only 20. And it was the old Jack again, buying round after round for his new friends and being hailed as the grandest of people in all

London. In four hours he went from being obliging to being obliterated.

He woke up in his hotel bedroom the next morning, without any idea of how he had gotten there. His pain soon gave way to shame. How could he have fallen so far so quickly? How could he have gone from following Jesus on the King's Highway to jumping back into the miry sludge of the forsaken ditch he'd seen in his vision. He was convinced at the time that what happened last night would never happen again. He had committed to a life of following Jesus so closely that if He suddenly stopped, Jack would bump into Him. To Jack, a lifetime of sobriety was his destiny.

But now, here he was, lost without hope, adrift in a sea of dangerous waves pounding him down, down, down. Where would he go now? How could he face Marianne? What about his job? The chink in his armor was so large that Satan gained a foothold into his mind. "The Charing Cross Tube Station is only ten minutes away and trains pass through there every five minutes. You can jump down into the tracks and all your problems will be gone."

There comes a time in the lives of well over one million Americans each year when life seems so hopeless they attempt the final solution. Fifty thousand of them succeed. Jack was about to be one of those two statistics, most likely a victorious suicide when you jump in front of something as big as a train.

"Yes, suicide," Jack whispered to the reflection in the bathroom mirror that he hardly recognized as himself. "I can't go on any longer this way. There's no hope for me; I'm a loser. Even God has abandoned me. I tried to follow Him but failed miserably. The world will be better off without me."

At first, tears ran down his cheeks. Then he experienced a feeling of exhilaration when he firmly decided he would indeed follow through on letting a train bring his miserable life to an end.

He put on his best suit, left the hotel, and off he went toward Charing Cross. When he arrived at the station, he heard a still, small voice in his mind say, "No! Walk three minutes south on Strand Street to Trafalgar Square and I will minister to you there."

It's strange, at times, what the Holy Spirit puts into our minds to guide us and protect us. He brought to Jack's remembrance a particular football game of the past season. The Vikings were behind 33 points at halftime and walked into the locker room hearing boos from their fans and the muttering of players saying all was lost and they'd just as soon not go back out there in the second half. The other team was too good for them. Then one voice from a respected defensive star rose above the rest and said, "We can beat this team. We won't let them score in the second half and all we need to do is score seven touchdowns." The players listened and believed. They didn't quite hold the other team scoreless—they made one field goal —but the Vikings scored 39 points and won the game.

That's what happened to Jack. All his negative thoughts and the voice that told him to jump in front of a train at Charing Cross were muffled by the powerful voice that told him to go to Trafalgar Square and He'd minister to him there. He made it to Trafalgar Square in exactly three minutes. His eye was drawn to the 170-foot column and statue of Admiral Horatio Nelson across the plaza from where he entered the square.

There were few people in the plaza at mid-morning on a foggy day. In the haze, Jack could barely make out that there was a single person standing in front of Nelson's Column. He started across the plaza toward that one person, as if he were a magnet and Jack a metal object. As the distance between them lessened, Jack became more and more mesmerized by the somebody before him. He was about six feet tall and had a sturdy athletic build with broad back. His hands were large and strong, like those of a football player. He had curly dark brown hair, medium cut, and was wearing what looked to be his best suit.

"Manny!" Jack shouted out. "What are you doing here?"

"Are you surprised to see me, Jack?" Manny answered.

As the sun rises in the morning and lightens up a world of darkness, Jack experienced a beam of light in his mind that removed the scales from his mind's eye and gave him hope that a whole new day for him would be dawning. Manny had that effect on him.

"No, Manny, I'm really not surprised to see you. I would have been surprised if you hadn't been here. I realize that everything today has been drawing me toward this very moment. You know how much I need you right now, don't you?" Jack stated.

"I do," Manny replied with a voice that seemed like a lifeline to Jack. "Are you ready for your final lesson."

Jack wondered what Manny meant by "the final lesson," but he knew he'd find out in not too long.

"Yes, Manny, I'm ready for the final lesson."

The Final Lesson

It was unusual for the two of them to be standing in front of Nelson's Column for more than an hour without anyone being exactly where they were, even though there were now at least a hundred people in the plaza of Trafalgar Square. It was as if there were an invisible fence built around them.

Jack waited for Manny to start the final lesson, but he didn't. It was awkward, like a professor walking into a classroom filled with alert and waiting students, and standing mute at the podium until one of them asked a question. Today, in Trafalgar Square, Jack was that student.

After half a minute, Jack broke the silence. "What happened to me, Manny? I've been following Jesus with all my heart. I've been studying the Bible every day like you taught me and praying like you showed me."

Jack took several minutes more to update Manny on all the following-Jesus things he was doing, including being involved in a Christian shelter for the homeless in a less traveled part of town.

At the end of his recitation, Manny still said nothing. He just looked at Jack with those piercing eyes.

Jack took the cue and continued on. "Manny, I made the commitment to follow Jesus every step of the way. I even had a vision of following Jesus." He recalled that entire vision to Manny, word for word as he had recorded it in his spiritual journal.

Jack stopped, as if he were searching for just the right words to express his frustration with it all. Then he spoke with the voice of a person trying to figure out why his best friend had ghosted him.

"I mean, what more could I have done than to seek for Jesus with all my heart and know Him like the back of my hand? What am I missing, Manny?"

That was the question Manny had waited for to launch the lesson. After all, how can teachers teach until they know what it is their students don't understand?

"So, you think you know Jesus. Is that it Jack? But do you really know Him—in an intimate way? Not as a thought in your mind but as a presence in your innermost being, in that place you call me? Do you know Him there?"

Manny paused. Jack held his breath. "There's one vital thing you've been missing, Jack. It's like your breathing in air with half the oxygen. You've been devoted to a concept of Jesus ahead of you and your following Him. You've felt that the more you know about Him, the easier it will be to follow Him, even if He leads you into the valley of the shadow of death. That's a worthy undertaking, and I applaud you for it. Nevertheless, Jack, you fall short in one matter. You've been dealing with a something and not a Someone."

Manny may as well have been speaking that last sentence to Jack in a coded language.

Jack scratched his head and fumbled for words. Finally, out came an exasperated and short-winded question, like a plea from someone trying to crawl out of the deep ditch alongside the King's Highway and exhausted by the effort. "What're you talking about, Manny?" That's as coherent a question as Jack could muster up.

"I'm talking about Jesus in you and you in Him," Manny said. "Not a concept of Jesus in your mind but the real Jesus."

Jack had the look of a student in an Introduction to Accounting class trying to figure out the difference between a debit and a credit.

"I don't understand the Someone and not something, Manny."

"I know you don't, Jack. If you did, you wouldn't have fallen from sobriety as you did last night. And as you'll fall again in the future when you make decisions in the blink of an eye. Make no mistake about it, Jack. You're in a battle with an enemy who wants to destroy you, and you're not equipped to fight him with a concept of Jesus."

Jack was starting to feel like he had that morning when Satan told him to jump in front of a train. Manny could see his head droop and his shoulders slope downward.

"So there's nothing I can do to reclaim my life?" Jack managed to whimper out.

Compassion swept over Manny, like a mother sitting by the bedside of her ailing child through the long night. "Jack, you're right. There's nothing you can do under your own power to stay sober for the rest of your life. You demonstrated that decisively last night. All your efforts to follow Jesus and fight your demons with Him beside you failed when you encountered something you hadn't anticipated. Addiction is a terrible thing, Jack. Some people are able to stop drinking or using drugs through an almost fanatical dedication, like a weight-lifter who trains until he wins an Olympic medal in the snatch and lift. You're not one of those people—few are."

When Manny observed the look of dejection on Jack's face, he knew he had to move quickly to the positive.

"Do you remember we started our lessons by talking about finding the safest place on earth?" Manny asked.

It was a rhetorical question, but it caught Jack's attention. If there was one thing Manny could have said to pull Jack away from the path of a fast-moving train, that sentence did it. Jack nodded his head as if he'd just been handed a lifeline where he stood in the miry sludge at the bottom of the steep ditch.

Manny continued. "Listen carefully Jack. The safest place on earth is not an abstraction or a concept, not a thought in your mind or a sudden revelation, not even being in the Bible or in prayer or in Christian service.

"I'll say it once more, my friend. Write it in your mind with indelible ink. It's not a something but a Someone. And the Bible says that Someone is within you, the Spirit of the actual Jesus.

"You see, Jack, you expect Jesus to keep you from drinking because you've committed your life to following Him. Your mistake, however, is that you've been following your idea of Jesus rather than who He really is. You have a shadowy picture of God and why Jesus came and what your relationship to Him should be. You need to allow the light of Jesus to come flooding in and disperse the shadow. You need to be nourished by Jesus Himself, as if you were taking in His very flesh and blood."

Jack struggled to understand Manny, like a beginning swimmer in choppy water. "You're going way beyond my ability to follow you, Manny. Can you please give me a picture to help me?"

"Let me give you a Bible verse to show you what I mean by taking in Jesus." He handed Jack a Bible from his briefcase. "Turn to John 6." When Jack did so, verse 56 was highlighted.

> Those who eat my flesh and drink my blood
> live in me, and I live in them.

Manny caught the queasy look on Jack's face. "I can see by your face that you've a reaction much like many of the disciples present when He said that. It's a hard teaching to be sure." Jack noticed another highlight four verses later.

> When many of Jesus' disciples heard him,
> they said, "What he says is hard to accept. Who
> wants to listen to him anymore?"

"It *is* a hard teaching, Manny. It sounds like cannibalism. I've read these verses before and kind of skipped over them because I'm obviously not getting what Jesus meant. I know He's not talking about eating His actual flesh and drinking His actual blood."

"You're right, Jack. He's not talking about cannibalism. But He is talking about feeding on Him, taking in his life to receive all He is and all He can do in you. Blood represents the life of a creature and bread the sustenance of life. What He's really saying is that all His followers need to take Him into their very selves—His real presence, symbolized by His flesh and blood—if they are to be fully alive and safe. Not an idea of Him, no matter how noble. There's nothing more real than flesh and blood."

At this point, Jack interrupted Manny. "I'm beginning to see it, I think. But couldn't Jesus have made the same point in a less gruesome way?"

Manny smiled. "Oh, but He did Jack. Anything as important as living in Christ and Him living in you as the consummation of the Christian life will most certainly be found elsewhere. Move yourself nine chapters further to John 15." Once again, one verse was highlighted, the fourth one.

> "Live in me, and I will live in you. A branch cannot produce any fruit by itself. It has to stay attached to the vine. In the same way, you cannot produce fruit unless you live in me."

"During His life on earth, the words Jesus chiefly used when speaking of the relationship between Him and the disciples with Him were: 'Follow Me.' Now that He was about to leave them, He gave them a new message that was much more intimate and personal, a message that meant a spiritual union with Himself. He invited them to 'Live in Me.'

"There's nothing wrong with following Jesus, Jack. Lots of Christians take that path, and that's good enough to keep them solid in their faith. They're taking a high road, but it's not the highest road—living in Christ is. It's different for you, Jack, than the average Christian. You're an addict, and you need something stronger than following Jesus to stay sober.

"I'm going to give you an analogy that may seem a bit odd to you because you're an alcoholic. I'm using it because you, of all people, will understand it completely. If you want to get intoxicated, you won't get to that point by pouring a thimbleful of whiskey into a mixed drink. You'll put in a shot or a double-shot or just drink the whiskey straight. Now instead of getting intoxicated on alcohol, you want to be high on Jesus, and you don't get there by thimblefuls of Him. You get there by drinking as close to straight Jesus as you can, and that only happens if you let the full presence of Him be active in you. As a Christian, you always have Jesus in you, but you determine the mixture between His kingdom and the world, between Him and you, and between Him and the enemy."

Jack had to chuckle when Manny gave him the picture of drinking straight Jesus. At a different time, he might have laughed, but this was a guy who not too long ago had been willing to jump in front of a train.

"That did it Manny! Now I see what John 6:56 means and the vine and the branch and all the rest of it."

Jack felt like he'd just downed six fingers of Jesus and looked up at Admiral Nelson. He felt like he'd been given a secret of the Christian life. Then a whisper crept into his mind telling him he didn't have the full revelation of the matter.

"I've got the feeling we're not done yet, Manny, that there's something else."

"There's always something else, Jack," Manny said with a twinkle in his eyes. "Even when you take the real Jesus into your inner being, the part of you that you call 'me,' He looks around and says, 'It's too crowded in here for Me, Jack.'"

That *huh* look was pasted on Jack's face once more.

"I've lost you again, haven't I?" Manny ventured. If you count tossing a person into the middle of a dense forest as being lost, Jack was indeed lost.

"Within your inner being—what is called your soul—there are three realities: Jesus, you, and the natural world. That's what He means by it being too crowded. He doesn't want equal billing with Jack and the world. John the Baptist said, 'He must become greater; I must become less.' He's the star of the show; nothing less than that will do."

Jack scratched his head and said, "I need another picture to catch what you're saying."

Right on cue, Manny gave him the picture.

"Open the Bible in your hand to Matthew 9:17."

Jack did so and read.

> Neither do people pour new wine into old wineskins. If they do, the skins will burst; the wine will run out and the wineskins will be ruined. No, they pour new wine into new wineskins, and both are preserved."

"Jack, this verse speaks directly to you. The old wineskin

is the Jack who has too high of a billing in the drama of your life. Then there's everything going on in the world around you —hurricanes in Florida, politics, wars in the Middle East, the big football game on Sunday, and your neighbor tossing his grass clippings in the street.

"You've been pouring lots of the new wine of Jesus into your wineskin as you've been following Him and seeking Him with all your heart. That's a good thing. But when you add more of Jack and the world into the wineskin, it will burst. That's what happened to you at the retirement party last night. There was too much of you and wanting to please all the people there in your wineskin. However much of Jesus there was in you burst out at the first toast, and it all went downhill from there."

The place where they were standing became so still that several quiet coughs forty feet away sounded like a drum roll. By now, Jack knew Manny wasn't finished yet.

After thirty seconds, enough time for Jack to reflect on what had just been said, Manny filled in the picture. "You are the old wineskin, all worn and stretched out by a lifetime of listening to the world and going your own way for most of your life. You've been trying to store Jesus alongside everything else in you. That may work for a while, but then something happens and the wineskin bursts and your new-found trusting in Jesus and following Him forever pours out on the ground."

Jack felt so low that he'd need rock-climbing techniques to scale a curb. "What do I do then, Manny? It seems there's no hope for me."

"Turn back to the verse you read in Matthew, Jack. I want you to read the last sentence, but skip the first two words and read the next six."

Jack did so.

Pour new wine into new wineskins.

"There's your hope, Jack, direct from the mouth of Jesus. He knows your struggles with addiction, He knows what your life was like before He came into it, and He has the answer. He also knows that you can't fit the new Him into the old you. You need a transfusion, like what happens to someone with a blood disease. The old blood needs to be pumped out before the new blood can flow in. You need to put aside your old self-centered self and your allegiance to the ways of the world. But you can't do that on your own; self can't diminish self.

"You've already found that saying no to alcohol doesn't work long term. That's because you have an addictive personality. The bad news is that you'll die with an addictive personality—it's so much a part of you. The good news is that you can change your addiction. Instead of alcohol, you can be addicted to Jesus. You can let Him govern your life instead of yourself."

Manny handed Jack a note card. "Here's an important prayer for you, Jack. Please read it out loud."

Jack did so.

> Lord Jesus, as of right now, I give You my mind to think with, my will to decide, and my emotions to react.

"That's the new wine in the new wineskin Jack—Jesus in place of your old self and the fallen world. Yours becomes a surrendered self, not a self-seeking and influenced-by-the-world self or a self which is vulnerable to the temptations of Satan. Colossians 1:27 becomes your mantra.

> Christ in you, the hope of glory.

"That's the picture to focus on—Jesus, the new wine, flowing into a heart and surrendered soul prepared and waiting for Him to take over, the new wineskin as it were. The old you is gone; the new you has come.

"You've been battling your addiction for many years. You've prayed for Jesus to keep you from drowning in alcohol. You should have been praying for the Holy Spirit to shrink Jack and the world to make room for Jesus."

Jack was no longer at the bottom of a curb. He stood straight and tall. "Now I see it. I've been trying to put the new wine of Jesus into the old wineskin of Jack. That old wineskin burst at the retirement party, and it will burst again when I least expect it. Satan is lurking just around the corner to trip me up, and I'm vulnerable because there's too much of Jack and the world in Jack. I need one more explanation Manny."

"Of course, Jack," Manny responded. "I'll bet it has to do with being filled with Jesus through the Holy Spirit."

A grandmaster in chess understands his opponent's next three moves even before he does. That's the way it was with Manny. He knew what Jack was going to say before Jack even thought it.

With a wry smile on his face, Jack said. "Yes, Manny, that's what I was going to ask about. Why do you even bother to wait for me to ask a question or make a comment. You know what it's going to be anyway. Why not just continue on without my remarks?"

Manny was prepared for that observation. "Because, Jack, it's important for you to hear your own voice."

Jack chose not to ask him what he meant by that. It would only be a diversion to the final lesson.

Jack spoke slowly and haltingly, so as to make sure he was stating his case clearly and completely. "We've talked about being filled with the Holy Spirit or not being filled with the Holy Spirit. Now you've introduced the idea that I can have more of Jesus in me or less of Him, especially if I'm giving equal space to myself and the world. Is there only part of the Holy Spirit in me that I need to be filled with the rest of Him? And is there only part of Jesus in me that I need more of Him?"

Manny rubbed his hands together, as a ray of sunlight crossed his face like a harbinger of what he was about to bring to Jack's question. "No, Jack, the Holy Spirit is fully in you, all of Him, all the time. And it's the same way with Jesus."

"I believe what you're saying because I trust you to tell me only the truth, but could you paint one last picture for me. I hear it but I can't see it." Jack rubbed his eyes. "Does that make sense?" Jack asked.

"It makes perfect sense, Jack," Manny replied. "Jesus used parables to paint pictures of what he meant so His disciples could learn his teaching clearly.

"That's what *you* need—a parable."

Jack's eyes moved up and to the right to prepare for the visual image he was about to receive. "Which parable in the Bible will we be looking at?" he asked.

"It's not a parable in the Bible, Jack," Manny pointed out. "It's my own parable."

Manny went to a page in his book of parables that he kept on a library shelf in his mind.

"Let's say you're sitting in a pew in a Spirit-filled church on Easter Sunday, and the Holy Spirit is pushing out the walls with His presence. It seems like the praise and worship music is straight from the halls of heaven, and the pastor preaches a sermon on the resurrection that puts Jesus so firmly into the minds of most attenders that they lose track of who *they* are."

"That's what all of the Holy Spirit and all of Jesus means. Do you have the picture so far, Jack?"

Jack didn't hesitate. "I do, Manny, but ..." Manny held up his hand to stop Jack from saying anything more.

"I'll take care of the but, Jack," Manny instructed him. It was like a teacher telling a student that he wasn't done with his illustration yet, and Manny wasn't.

"But you're sitting there filled with your own thoughts —the golf game you played yesterday, the disagreement with your wife that morning, the presentation coming up with a client who's expressed serious reservations about a state-of-the-art defibrillator, the stupid thing a senator said about taxation, the conflict going on in the Middle East, the latest wildfire in California, and a hundred other things that have to do with you and the world you live in.

"Do you see it? You are that church, Jack, from wall to wall, from the front to the back. The Holy Spirit and Jesus are fully in you, but you're paying little or no attention to them. Instead, you're filled with Jack and the world you live in. Jesus and the Holy Spirit are in you fully, as is the Father, but you are not fully in tune with the triune God."

Finally, with that parable, Jack got it. He finally got it! He really got it! Following Jesus was not the highest road for him. Being in Jesus was. In the church of his soul, he needed to shut out Jack and the world as best he could and let Jesus, through the power of the Holy Spirit, be his all in all.

Jack's could hardly contain his excitement. "I see it, Manny. I do see it. At long last, I see it, and I see why this is the final lesson." That was a lot of seeing, and Jack realized there was no lesson needed beyond this one.

Jack had one critical profession to make. "I have faith that the Bible is true, completely. If God's Word says that Jesus is actually and fully within me, then He is."

"Then what are you going to do about it?" Manny asked in a gentle voice.

Jack hesitated, but not for more than a few seconds. "You've told me I can't do anything about it under my own willpower. I can only have a disposition to listen for Jesus within me and seek His guidance."

"So you will seek His guidance?"

"Yes."

"How will you do that?"

Again, there was a short pause. "Hmm," Jack said, "Since He's within me, I guess I'll just ask Him."

"Good answer," Manny replied. "If Jesus is within you—and He is—why would you not ask Him about everything?"

"Why not, indeed," Jack said. "If I'd asked Him about going to the retirement party instead of making the decision on the spur of the moment, He'd have told me not to go because He'd have known what would happen. I didn't."

Manny looked as pleased as a shepherd rescuing a sheep from a lion or a bear, as King David did, and bringing it back to the safety of his sheep pen.

"That's it, Jack!" he said. "You throw away your old wineskin filled with Jack and the things of this world, and you carry within you a new wineskin made to be filled with Jesus, one that will stretch as you pour in more and more of Jesus.

"And you ask the Jesus in your new wineskin about everything, both great and small, instead of thinking your own thoughts and making your own decisions.

"If you do those two things, you won't drink again. You need the real Jesus within your soul throwing the punches to keep Satan out. Without that you can't defend yourself. Following Him on the outside hasn't been enough for you. You need Him on the inside, Jack."

Jack knew in his heart that what Manny said would keep him sober if he made those two things the foundation of his life, without exceptions.

Manny became like a minister who turns to the congregation for the final blessing. "It's time to end our time together with a prayer to serve as the glue for your living in Christ, being a new wineskin, and asking Jesus about everything.

> "Lord Jesus, I surrender to You today, desiring your Holy Spirit to rule my life, wanting You to fulfill Your mighty powers through me.
>
> I acknowledge You in all my ways, leaning not on my own understanding but trusting you with all my heart, giving You my mind to think with, my will to decide, my emotions to react.
>
> As of right now, I allow You, Lord Jesus, to govern my behavior wherever it may be – at home, at work, in recreation, alone or with others, at rest – rejoicing in the glorious fact that You live within me, sharing Your life with me, communicating that life to me in the nitty-gritty process of being and living 24 hours a day.
>
> Your breath in my lungs, Your words on my lips, Your smile on my face. Your vision through my eyes, Your understanding through my ears, Your touch with my hands.
>
> What a marvelous thing – abiding like a branch on the vine, letting the vine bear the fruit through the branch. This is my prayer today, heavenly Father and precious Savior. Quicken me to live it out, Your Spirit to my spirit, every minute of this day."

Jack sat in awe. He had just heard a prayer that would start every day of his life for the rest of his time on earth. He knew now that he would never drink again, not because of anything he could do but because his life would be a reflection that Jesus was living in Him and taking care of him and doing what Jack himself could never do. He also knew that it would take time to feed on Jesus to become strong in the Spirit and to grow into Jesus the Vine. And He knew in His heart that He would take the time. That's the one thing he could do; the rest was up to Jesus.

The Best of Times

Jack drew his final line in the sand, one he would never cross again for the rest of his life. He was set free from the bondage to alcohol, like former prisoners whose felonies are expunged from all legal records, as if they'd never committed the crime in the first place.

As time went on, Jack became more and more like Jesus. How could he not? After all, Jesus was no longer a concept to follow but the Someone Jack saw in his mind, felt in his emotions, and surrendered to with his will. The wineskin within him had a very large Jesus who dominated his soul and a very small Jack and the world in the background. Sometimes, Jack even forgot about himself. Sometimes, the world became so distant in the background that he lost track of it.

Prayer became a smaller amount of talking and a larger degree of listening. Life became less of "How do I see it and what should I do here?" and more "How do You see it, Lord and what would You have me do here?" He never again read from the Bible without asking the Holy Spirit to reveal the truths and promises of the Word of God. One of his life verses, in addition to John 6:56 and 15:4, became James 1:1, in a personalized rendition.

> Jack, a servant of God and of the Lord Jesus Christ.

He served his Lord and Master, not because he had promised to do so but because he wanted to serve Him, with all his heart and all his soul and all his strength. God's will became his will. What God wanted him to do with his life, he gladly did.

After Jack retired from his company, he became a respected elder in his church and altruist in his community. He became the director of a homeless community and ministered to drug addicts and alcoholics who had given up all hope. Over a period of 18 years, he helped more than 30 people stop drinking or using drugs. In a way, he became their Manny.

At the age of 84, Jack died peacefully in his sleep with his family surrounding him, having found the safest place on this earth and now fully alive in the absolute and unsurpassed safety of heaven. Hundreds of people came to his funeral to pay their respects for a life well lived in service to his Creator and to them. But his reception on earth was nothing compared to his reception in heaven, where His Lord and Savior welcomed him with these glorious words, "Well done, good and faithful servant!"

The End

CPSIA information can be obtained
at www.ICGtesting.com
Printed in the USA
JSHW012338110423
40175JS00003B/200